MISCHIEF GOES SOUTH

H. W. TILMAN

Mischief close reefed in Drake Passage

MISCHIEF
GOES SOUTH

H. W. TILMAN

TILMAN

First published 1968 by Hollis & Carter Ltd
This edition published 2016 by Tilman Books
www.tilmanbooks.com
a joint venture by
Lodestar Books www.lodestarbooks.com
and Vertebrate Publishing www.v-publishing.co.uk

Cover design by Jane Beagley
Vertebrate Graphics Ltd. www.v-graphics.co.uk

Lodestar Books has asserted their right
to be identified as the Editor of this Work

Series editor Dick Wynne
Series researcher Bob Comlay

The publisher has made reasonable effort to locate
the holders of copyright in the illustrations in this book,
and will be pleased to hear from them regarding
correct attribution in future editions

A CIP catalogue record for this book
is available from the British Library

ISBN 978-1-909461-32-1

Typeset in Baskerville from Storm Type Foundry
Printed and bound by Pulsio, Bulgaria
All papers used by Tilman Books are sourced responsibly

Contents

Photographs

Maps

Mischief

Bristol Channel Pilot Cutter built at Cardiff 1906 by Thos. Baker, East Canal Wharf. Length 45 feet. Beam 13 feet. Draught 7 feet 6 inches. Net tons 13.78. T.M. 29 tons.

1906–1919	Working pilot boat owned by William Morgan or 'Billy the Mischief'	
1920	Sold for £450 to a Mr Unna who sailed her to Takoradi	
1927	First appears in the Yacht Register and had subsequently in 27 years ten different owners	
1954	Bought at Malta by Ernle Bradford who sailed her to Palma, Mallorca and sold her to her last owner, H. W. Tilman	
1954	Palma—Gibraltar—Oporto—Lymington	2000 m.
1955–56	Las Palmas—Monte Video—Magellan Straits—Valparaiso—Callao-Panama—Bermuda—Lymington (*Mischief in Patagonia*, 1957)	20,000 m.
1957–58	Las Palmas—Bahia Blanca—C. Town—Durban—Beira—Comoro Is.—Aldabra—Aden—Port Said—Malta—Gibraltar—Lymington (*Mischief Goes South*, 1968)	21,000 m.
1959–60	Las Palmas—C. Town—lies Crozet—Kerguelen—C. Town—St Helena—Lymington (*Mischief Among The Penguins*, 1961)	20,000 m.
1961	West Greenland. Godthaab—Umanak Fjord—Godthaab—Lymington (*Mischief in Greenland*, 1964)	7500 m.
1962	West Greenland. Godthaab—Evighedsfjord—Holsteinborg—Exeter Sound (Baffin Is.)—Lymington (*Mischief in Greenland*, 1964)	6500 m.
1963	Baffin Bay. Godthaab—Godhaven—Upernivik—Lancaster Sound—Bylot Is.—Pond Inlet—Godthaab—Lymington (*Mostly Mischief*, 1966)	6500 m.

Surveyed Dec. 1963 and reported no longer fit for long voyages.

1964	East Greenland: Faroe Is.—Reykjavik— Angmagssalik—Lymington (*Mostly Mischief*, 1966)	3700 m.
1965	East Greenland: Reykjavik—Angmagssalik— Skjoldungen—Lymington (*Mostly Mischief*, 1966)	4000 m.
1966–67	Las Palmas—Montevideo—Punta Arenas— South Shetland Is.—South Georgia—Montevideo —Azores—Lymington (*Mischief Goes South*, 1968)	20,400 m.

Two mountains and a cape have officially been named after her—Mont du Mischief, by the French, on Île de la Possession, Îles Crozet; Cap MMischief, also by the French, on Île de Kerguelen; Mount Mischief, by the Canadian Survey, Exeter Sound, Baffin Is. near to Mt. Raleigh.

The author gratefully acknowledges permission to quote from the following publications: From Frank Bullen's *The Cruise of the Cachalot*, by courtesy of Collins Publishers; from the author's *Mischief in Patagonia*, by courtesy of the Cambridge University Press; from Hugh Kingsmill's *Invective and Abuse*, by courtesy of Eyre & Spottiswoode Ltd; from a number of Admiralty Pilots, by courtesy of H.M. Stationery Office; from L. P. Kirwan's *The White Road*, by courtesy of Hollis & Carter Ltd; from *Lecky's Wrinkles in Practical Navigation*, by courtesy of George Philip & Son Ltd; from a paper read by Dr Dilwyn John to the Royal Geographical Society, by courtesy of the Royal Geographical Society; and from an article by Charles Douglas-Home, by courtesy of *The Times*.

Foreword

Skip Novak

B ILL TILMAN. It seems I have been trailing in his wake for the last three decades...

In the summer of 1983 I was invited to 'boat captain' the sixty-one-foot sloop *War Baby* for her voyage to Scandinavia and the Arctic. The owner/skipper Warren Brown was a renowned ocean racer and blue water cruiser. In fact, *War Baby* was a famous racing boat that, as a young lad, I had crewed on in the 1972 Transatlantic Race from Bermuda to Bayona, Spain. At the age of 20, and well before satellite navigation, let alone GPS, I made it a point to understudy the navigator and learned the art and science of celestial navigation en route. Before I realised it I was destined to spend more than a fair share of my life at sea girdling the globe on various around-the-world races and other ocean passages, that eventually overlapped with a long career in expedition sailing to high latitudes that continues to this day.

By the time of our cruise north in 1983 I had been based on the south coast of the UK for seven years and had two Whitbread Round the World Races under my belt. I was still footloose and fancy free, leaving a trail of failed relationships astern in my blind ambition for wild places by land and sea—living out of a sea bag ready for any adventure at a moment's notice.

For *War Baby*'s cruise, we prepped from Lymington. One of my responsibilities, in addition to modifying and equipping a former race boat for her cruise north, was to compile a library of Arctic literature pertinent to our itinerary. This is when I first discovered Bill Tilman's *Triumph and Tribulation*, realising with regret that back in the mid to late 1970s I had probably passed by him on the dockside in Lymington.

Was it a golden opportunity lost, or a blessing in disguise that I had neither met him nor seen his well-known adverts for crew that promised "no pay, no prospects and not much pleasure"? I might have been in time to sign on for his ill-fated East Greenland expedition with *Baroque*. In fact, given the time frame, I might have ended up on *En Avant*... along with the young crew including the 79-year old Bill Tilman, never to be seen again after their stop in Rio de Janeiro on the way to the Antarctic in 1977.

You see, in addition to being a professional sailor, I was a keen and frustrated mountaineer. Had I encountered Bill and started a gam, it would have been more than likely I would have been invited on board for his next expedition—and might have enjoyed what he called on one voyage his "fine view of the Isle of Wight through the port side planking," of his Bristol Channel Pilot Cutter taking leave of the UK for the great unknown.

During my high latitude baptism on *War Baby* in 1983, in the space of four months we had visited the Scilly Isles, made a pub crawl in Howth, Ireland (where I fell in love yet again), sampled the liquid production in the Western Isles, made a whistle stop tour of the Norwegian coast from Bergen to Hammerfest, trekked across Bear Island (stupidly without a bear gun), and cruised the north-west and north coasts of Spitsbergen before returning to the UK via the Faroe Islands.

Contingent on taking the job in hand, I was promised that our objectives were to land people to explore inland, which would include some serious trekking, camping and climbing within the abilities of a mixed group. In spite of making every effort to climb every bit of high ground possible (although not necessarily before breakfast as Tilman might have advocated), the schedule was rushed with the owner's guests coming and going at various ports along the way. Deadlines prevailed. We did manage to camp on the beach known as Gravenset (sealer's graves) in Magdalena Fjord and we climbed where we thought Tilman had climbed in 1974 , but by and large the voyage was a frustration of too much ocean covered in too short a time and a raft of missed objectives in the hills. Let it be said it was an introduction to the possibilities, and for that I was thankful. Through my obsessions with high ground I was nicknamed 'Tilman' by the crew, which suited me just fine.

The result of that foray and the solution to my dilemma was simply to build my own boat. In 1987 I launched my first expedition vessel

Pelagic, specifically to sail to remote areas to climb. Over the next three decades the Tilman stories would serve as inspiration to our travels in Patagonia, Spitsbergen, Antarctica and South Georgia. The shipmates who were with me back then all became, and continue to be, Tilman aficionados able to come up with a Tilman one liner, witticism or some sage advice, *ad lib*. One of our favorites is always "Every herring should hang by his own tail," of which the meaning is very clear—self-sufficiency is key and don't expect a bail-out, if you go adventuring. Indeed, on our travels it became a priority to visit as many of the sites, described in the books with typical Tilman style and humour, of several mishaps or near disasters. *Mischief in Patagonia* which describes his first foray afloat to Chile in 1955–56 provides a surfeit of material.

Anyone who has brought a small boat alongside a jetty or left it and made a hash of the job in front of spectators will no doubt relate to how he described the "aquatic sports" of getting *Mischief* off the jetty at Punta Arenas, which included a jib dropped overboard, a grounding, an engine that wouldn't start and being rammed by a Chilean cruiser trying to help. Tilman, an observer of human nature *par excellence*, summed it up: "It was a Saturday afternoon and one could almost hear the happy sigh of the crowd as they realised how wise they had been to spend it on the jetty."

In Peel Inlet on the west coast of Chile more trouble ensued at the junction of the Calvo Fjord: "I was steering and elected to pass between two of the biggest [icebergs] which were some fifty yards apart. Although we were watching them pretty intently, for they seemed to be unusually still, it was not until we were up to them that I realised they were aground. A moment later we joined them." Having also done a lot of exploratory navigation in Chile, rather than being critical of Tilman's methods, that to a yachtsman would seem irresponsible and cavalier, we on the other hand could empathise. We had our share of groundings, but in the relating afterwards, they were never so cleverly described.

Further on at the north arm of Peel Inlet is Tilman Island, the scene of the infamous grounding when Tilman, Jorge Quinteros and Charles Marriot were crossing the Southern Patagonian Icecap to Lago Argentino. Bill Proctor had been left in charge of *Mischief* with John Van Tromp and Michael Grove aboard, and as Tilman relates it,

"Enough has been said of the extreme north end of Peel Inlet to show that it must be a fascinating place, and apparently Proctor's curiosity to see it proved irresistible." Nigh on three and a half tonnes of ballast in pig iron had to be extracted from the bilges and rowed ashore at slack water as they were grounded in a tidal race. After many mishaps and close calls in just staying on station, they managed to float off and then reship the ballast before taking shelter in Sea Lion Bay. We had spent two weeks there in 1993 attempting the unclimbed Mt Aguilera on the Wilcox Peninsula, and in view of the horrendous weather, which is typical, we had time to study and contemplate this debacle in its entirety. It is an accolade that in spite of what could have been the expedition's undoing, not to mention leaving the three stranded on the beach in the Calvo Fjord, Tilman, instead of making a meal of it, dismissed and forgave Proctor's folly with that single sentence, perhaps realising his own methods all too well.

In 2004 on *Pelagic Australis* after another visit to Bear Island we managed to circumnavigate Spitsbergen and sailed through the Hinlopen Straits and into Freemansund, a channel between Barents and Edge Islands, a shortcut which has strong tidal currents. With too much ice on the outside of Edge Island Tilman opted for the channel, in his words, "thus setting the scene for another regrettable incident."

In short, hanging from a stern kedge, they had to jettison all the vessel's ballast overboard, being too far from shore to row it in. Ditto all the water. All this while being attacked by ice marching to and fro with the tide, risking their rudder and propeller and losing two anchors into the bargain. A spare mainsail weighing about 400 pounds was also thrown over. Tilman: "Normally I get a lot of harmless pleasure from throwing overboard superfluous gear. The mainsail might be included in that category, but certainly not the ballast."

Having lost all the ballast they had to ship onboard beach stone to retrim. A discussion ensued about how much weight in ballast could be achieved with stone in the space heretofore occupied by the pig iron. Various optimistic estimates were mooted, before crew member Andrew "invoked the aid of Archimedes" and with a spring balance and a bucket of water calculated that the stone would only achieve a quarter of the weight in pig iron. Tilman's response is one of my many favorites: "Nothing has an uglier look than reason when it is not on our side, and we hastened to tell Andrew what he could do with Archimedes and his bath water."

The Tilman stories are reread on a regular basis not only for amusement, but by way of reminding ourselves of our fallibility (mistakes are still made) and for the wisdom of not taking ourselves too seriously. Some ships carry the Bible, we carry Tilman, a continuous source of inspiration and entertainment.

From the perspective of a modern yachtsman who is now dependent on a variety of gadgets, and in view of so many near misses experienced by Tilman and his crews, you can understand how recent generations might discredit his methods at sea, some of which may, with hindsight, have been suspect. As a mountaineer he is easier to sympathise with as the struggles that exist today in the mountaineering world, mainly based around self reliance, are not much different from the ones he experienced. Through the climbing books his toughness is recognised and therefore the mistakes made at sea become irrelevant; from the climber's perspective, his maritime misadventures would naturally be dismissed as mere bagatelles. And this is where voyaging is so fundamentally different from mountaineering. Why? In Tilman's own words, "The perils of the sea are less apparent than the perils of climbing and have to be carefully assessed. In climbing the penalty for a mistake is obvious and is sometimes exacted instantaneously, so that on the whole there are far fewer foolish climbers than foolish amateur sailors."

I have often asked the question 'how would I have fared with this amateur sailor?' (by his own admission) while lurching from one mishap to another. In my younger days during Tilman's final years I might have ended up as many of his crew had done—stranded in a foreign port, considering themselves lucky to be onshore and alive. If we could turn back the clock, but not my age, given the chance I would have been stoic and survived, just for the privilege of being his shipmate.

Skip Novak
Cape Town
February 2016

Preface

WHILE THIS BOOK IS MAINLY a record of *Mischief*'s most recent voyage in 1966–67, I have included a hitherto unpublished account of an earlier voyage because there are features common to both. From my point of view both were failures. On the more recent one, though we reached our objective, we achieved nothing, and on the earlier one we did not reach our objective. On both voyages a man fell overboard, in one case with fatal consequences, and on both there was crew trouble. Happily on the earlier voyage this concerned only one man.

Writing about the recent voyage was like turning a knife in the wound. I had to exercise iron control. Instead of cheerfulness continually breaking in, as it should, plaintiveness and spleen were uppermost in my mind. But the latter do not make for either edifying or interesting reading. I have therefore suppressed my feelings and hope that the tone on the whole is moderate and the language of strictest reserve.

An anecdote of Swinburne told by Hugh Kingsmill in his book *Invective and Abuse* is relevant. Swinburne, who thought he had been affronted by Emerson, had written him a letter. 'I hope your language was quite moderate,' says his friend Gosse. 'Perfectly moderate,' replied Swinburne, 'I merely told him, in language of the strictest reserve, that he was a hoary-headed and toothless baboon, who, first lifted into notice on the shoulders of Carlyle, now spits and splutters from a filthier platform of his own finding and fouling. That is all I've said.'

H.W.T.
Barmouth
December 1967

PART ONE

---◆---

Islands of the Southern Ocean

July 1966–July 1967

Map 1: Track chart for Southern Ocean expedition: Lymington—Montevideo

CHAPTER I

THE OBJECTIVE AND THE CREW

W HAT ORNITHOLOGISTS, speaking *ex cathedra*, as it were, like to tell us about the habits of birds sometimes takes a lot of swallowing—an inelegant phrase, but apt enough in this context. For instance, one Forbush affirms in his whimsical way that the Arctic tern 'nests as far north as the most northern Eskimo live, while in winter its tireless pinions beat along the distant shore of unexplored lands of the Antarctic continent.' I am more willing to concede this because recently *Mischief*'s movements have been equally erratic, though less rapid, sailing off the east coast of Greenland in 1965, and in 1966 beating her tireless pinions far down in the Southern Ocean. With less compelling reasons than the Arctic tern has for its long journey, such behaviour may seem strange, especially after I had decided that from my point of view Greenland waters were the ideal cruising ground and that there was no need to look elsewhere. The point of view is important and since mine is not widely shared the following description of my ideal will be of help:

> A region to which the voyage is not too long, where Arctic waters beat upon coasts that are wild and little frequented, and that are studded with unclimbed mountains; where in summer one enjoys almost continuous daylight, the pale skies and soft colours of the north, and above all the romance and excitement of icebergs and pack-ice seen at close quarters from the deck of a small boat. A region where it is easy to imagine oneself in company with John Davis aboard his 50-ton ship *Mooneshine*, or with any of those hardy spirits, the Elizabethan seamen-explorers in search of a North-west passage.

A man must be allowed to change his mind. As Benedick remarked: 'When I said I would die a bachelor, I did not think I should live till I were married.' It is a mistake to get into a rut. Fired by the divine spark of discontent or out of cussedness, after five voyages to Greenland waters I felt in need of change. No doubt the most striking change would have been a cruise to the West Indies or the South Sea Islands, regarded as the Islands of the Blessed by most right-minded yachtsmen who, if they live in England, pine, not unreasonably, for sunshine, hula-hula girls, and bananas. Something could be said against such places but my main objection is that they have no mountains, or only mountains that are covered with a lush growth of tropical vegetation, suitable for bushwhackers but not for climbers. Instead my thoughts turned to the far South, to Antarctic islands; and since this would be a longer and more arduous undertaking than a Greenland voyage it was a case of now or never, before *Mischief* and her owner grew any older. Many would say, I suppose, that both should long since have been in a museum.

There, as in northern waters, one would enjoy the blessing of continuous daylight and would lack for nothing in the way of icebergs, glaciers, and mountains. Moreover, the Southern Ocean is richer in life—albatross, giant petrels, penguins, whales, seals, and sea elephants. Nor would romance be quite absent, though the sealers of the nineteenth century are not perhaps such heroic characters as the Elizabethan seamen-explorers. In Antarctic waters, lacking the incentive of an imagined North-west passage, exploration began at a more recent date; yet, even in the days of sail, many adventurous spirits found their way there, in search of a living rather than of fame.

Obviously a southern voyage has one or two drawbacks. The weather for one, which is likely to be ruder and colder, with a marked absence of the prolonged sunshine that is a heartening feature of the Greenland scene. Worse still is the great distance involved, a round journey of some 20,000 miles of twelve months' duration. *Mischief*'s earlier voyages had been to the South, to the Magellan Straits and Patagonian channels, and to the sub-antarctic islands of Crozet and Kerguelen. And of these I had said, misquoting Prince Hal: 'An intolerable deal of sea for one half-pennyworth of mountain.' The voyage I had in mind meant going farther south, to the South Shetland Islands, 500 miles south-east of Cape Horn and only some sixty miles from Graham Land, the northernmost tip of the Antarctic continent. This peninsula, by the way, whose name has long been in dispute between the Americans and ourselves—the Americans calling it Palmer Peninsula—is now known as the Antarctic Peninsula. The South Shetlands comprise eleven islands and in the *Antarctic Pilot* there is the following general description:

These islands were discovered by Mr W. Smith in the brig *Williams* on February 18th, 1819, when on a voyage from Buenos Aires to Valparaiso, and standing far to the southward. Smith again attempted to make the islands in June 1819 but met the pack-ice and had to abandon his project; but he succeeded during a third voyage in October of the same year, landing on King George Island. The commercial exploitation of the islands by numerous British and American sealers followed immediately upon their discovery. The valuable fur seals were taken in such numbers that by 1822 they were almost exterminated, though some sealing continued until 1828. During this period the coasts and harbours became well known and some of the early charts which were produced compare favourably with modern surveys.

The islands, which are largely volcanic, extend about 290 miles in an ENE and WSW direction between the parallels of 61° 00′ S. and 63° 22′ S. and the meridians of 53° 50′ W. and 62° 50′ W. and are separated by some navigable channels. The northern parts of the coasts of the islands abound with islets, rocks, and breakers, but the southern coasts are almost entirely clear of dangers. In the early part of spring the southern coasts are blocked with ice, which may also extend a considerable distance northwards from the islands during winter, making the islands inaccessible to vessels other than icebreakers.

The interior of the islands consists generally of high mountains, Smith Island (Lat. 63° 00′ S. Long. 62° 31′ W.) the highest, being 6900 feet high. The islands are almost entirely ice-covered all the year round, and it is only after midsummer (in January) that a few tracts which are free from snow carry lichens and mosses, in some places supplanted by small patches of grass. The summer may be compared with a mild British winter. Sea birds, principally penguins and petrels, are very plentiful as in the South Orkney Islands. Elephant seals are found on many of the beaches and their number appears to be increasing. Fur seals were abundant until their practical extermination during the nineteenth century. A few Weddell seals breed on the islands and the crab-eater seal is a rare visitor.

The particular island I had in my sights was naturally Smith Island, the most westerly of the group and the most mountainous. Livingston is the only other island of the group with mountains of interest. Smith Island has on it Mount Foster (6900 feet) and Mount Pisgah (6000 feet). Neither have been climbed. Indeed, so far as I can learn, no one has even landed on the island since James Weddell in 1820, a year after its discovery by William Smith. Many place-names in the Antarctic serve to remind us that sealers such as Smith, Weddell, Biscoe, Kemp, and Balleny were foremost in exploring those waters, prompted equally by a love of exploration and by the wish to find new, untouched sealing grounds. Weddell, a retired Master of the Royal Navy and a sealing captain, is famous for his penetration of the Weddell Sea in 1822 in the 160-ton brig *Jane* and the 65-ton cutter *Beaufroy*. In his *The White Road: A History of Polar Exploration* L. P. Kirwan writes:

> Weddell in his devotion to science was typical of these sealing captains of the first three decades of the nineteenth century. Despite the lack of proper instruments and the disgruntlement of his sailors at so apparently profitless an occupation, he did what he could, testing the direction and strength of currents, taking temperatures of the sea until his thermometers were smashed in a gale, puzzling over differences in magnetic variation, scrupulously observing even in moments of danger the nature, form, and movements of the ice. To persevere with such tasks in vessels cruelly exposed to the violence of Antarctic weather required a singular devotion. The experience of Weddell's ships on this lengthy pioneering voyage were not unusual. A whaleboat overboard, a rudder frozen into immobility; bulwarks, decks, and rigging so heavily encrusted with ice that the ship could scarcely rise to the sea—such experiences were common in the brigs and cutters of the Antarctic sealers in the early years of the nineteenth century.

No doubt Conrad had in mind more distant times, but the earlier years of the nineteenth century, at least in the Antarctic, might equally be included when he speaks of 'Days when the sea was great and mysterious, ready to surrender the prize of fame to audacious men.'

From my point of view, therefore, the South Shetlands were highly attractive—remote, inaccessible, mountainous. The fact that they were inhabited was a slight drawback. At least on one of them, Deception Island, there are British, Chilean, and Argentine bases. Smith Island offered a supreme challenge to the sea-going mountaineer, an even sterner challenge than that accepted recently by Warwick Deacock and his party of Australians and New Zealanders when they sailed to Heard Island in the sub-antarctic and climbed its 9000-foot peak Big Ben. For at Smith Island a party would be starting from scratch, without fore-knowledge of a possible landing place—there might well not be any—or of any route up the mountain. But apart from the island and its problems, the voyage alone would be an ambitious undertaking for an old 30-ton cutter with a skipper verging on the Psalmist's age limit. An old boat can, of course, be strengthened. But the man whose strength is diminished by age can only strive to emulate Beowulf's well known exhortation:

> Harder should be the spirit, the heart all the bolder,
> Courage the greater, as the strength grows less.

Ambitious or not, the voyage was within *Mischief*'s powers. Size is no criterion of a boat's seaworthiness. The sealers used to sail small boats in the Antarctic, but these were either carried there on the deck of the larger vessels or built on the spot. They did not try to sail them across Drake Passage, the stretch of water between Cape Horn and the South Shetlands. Edmund Fanning, an American sealer who was active in these waters, describes how he acquired a fleet of three such tenders, or shallops, as he calls them:

> Raising and decking our launch for one; then purchasing another which had in the previous season been built here by the crew of an English sealer; then taking the spare topmast of our vessel *Aspasia* for a keel, and a spare mainyard for a mast, together with some fifty oak knees roughly hewn that we had on board to support our battery

deck; with these materials and a number of 3-inch planks which had been used to floor the ballast over, and sundry articles purchased from the wreck of the *Regulator*, we proceeded to lay the keel of the third shallop on an iceberg, in a valley at the starboard side of the harbour. She was a first-rate seaboat, as well as the fastest sailer among the fleet.

The 'iceberg in a valley' is a puzzle. Does he mean an iceberg aground, or a glacier? And one would like to know why they laid the keel on an 'iceberg'. Was this the only flat ground available? Or was it to facilitate the launching? Or just for the hell of it?

Other than those built on the spot or carried there, no boat comparable to *Mischief* had sailed in Antarctic waters, much less crossed Drake Strait—with one memorable exception. Shackleton's famous do-or-die voyage from the South Shetlands to South Georgia in May, one of the worst weather months, is not likely ever to be forgotten. This voyage in the *James Caird*, a ship's lifeboat, was a rescue operation, a life or death matter, not only for the six men on board but for the other twenty-two men of the *Endurance* marooned on Elephant Island, the easternmost of the South Shetlands. Behind *Mischief*'s endeavour there would be no such compelling motive. The interest of the voyage itself and its ultimate aim must suffice to make it, as I thought, a worth-while undertaking. Anywhere at sea there are hazards, otherwise small-boat sailing would have less appeal. No waters are foolproof and Antarctic waters perhaps less so than any. As regards ice dangers, icebergs are visible even at night, and in low visibility one can always heave-to. Pack-ice we would avoid, for in summer the South Shetlands are normally ice-free. At Punta Arenas, through the Chilean navy, one could get reliable information about ice conditions, and if necessary wait there until the islands were reported free from ice. In summer a frigate or a naval tug plies frequently between Punta Arenas and the Chilean Antarctic bases.

The weather might have a more threatening aspect than the ice, but *Mischief*, in spite of her age, is staunch and a good seaboat, well able to stand up to the weather of those latitudes, the so-called Roaring Forties, Furious Fifties, and Shrieking Sixties. That is, of course, in summer conditions, between November and March. Ed Mikeska,

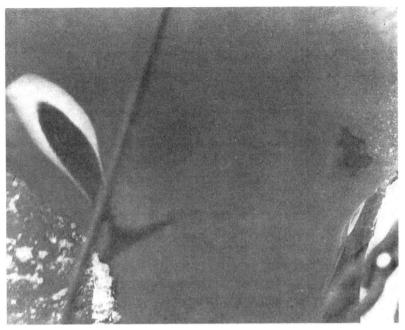

Commerson's dolphin underneath bowsprit shrouds, Magellan Straits; unidentified marine monster on right

North side of Neptune's Bellows, at the entrance to Port Foster, Deception Island

a professional seaman, who had sailed with me to Baffin Bay and who
had always regarded with apprehension *Mischief*'s, vulnerable skylight
and too roomy cockpit, wrote to me encouragingly in his own peculiar,
semi-seamanlike, staccato vein: 'I see you are to be a flying-fish sailor
again, Cape Horning? Going to spit to windward now! Have a couple
of good bilge-pumps fitted. Ole *Mischief*'s timbers will be a'shivering,
and mind yer blooming skylight, not to mention the snug, dry cockpit
you have. If you are lucky and hit a gale period in the South you will
make the Shetlands under bare poles and baggy-wrinkle.' But much
smaller boats than *Mischief* have successfully rounded Cape Horn.
One hoped that the weather might not be quite so fearful as has been
painted, and one knew that it does not become progressively worse farther south. In winter the weather could no doubt be hell, just as it can
be in the North Atlantic.*

     To find crews for *Mischief*'s first three voyages, which were all of
twelve months' duration, had involved me in much effort and trouble.
On the whole the results had been highly satisfactory so that none of
this effort had been wasted. There must be plenty of men of the right
stamp who would come forward if they knew what was afoot or if one
could make contact with them, but the publicity that could easily be
had and that would solve this problem is not all that welcome. One
would like to have the benefit without paying the degrading price, like
an American firm that proudly proclaims: 'We eschew publicity but we
know how to use it.' However, despite this desire to let things speak
for themselves, a policy that in these strident days might almost pass
for reticence, *Mischief*'s voyages have become better known. For each
succeeding voyage the need to shop around for crew or to advertise,

---

*   Note. Here is a specimen of winter Atlantic weather quoted recently in the
Meteorological Office publication, *The Marine Observer*. Trawler *St Barr*, Hull
to Labrador:

15th Feb. 1966	18.00	Wind WNW force 12, gusts to 87 knots, vis. 50 yds.
16th „ „	00.00	Wind NW force 11, snow, seas 35 ft. vis. 50 yds.
16th „ „	06.00	Wind NW force 11, continuous snow.
16th „ „	06.10	Wind NW increased and blew off wind-cups.
17th „ „	00.00	Wind NW force 11, main aerials down.
17th „ „	12.00	Wind NW force 7-8, snow showers, vis. 2½ miles.

became less. To find crews for her most recent voyages I had really exerted myself very little, merely lurking in my fastness behind the Welsh hills, vetting the letters of hopeful applicants, and sallying forth at intervals, like a spider from his web, to inspect and secure another victim. One had to take them on the principle of first come first served, for it was not reasonable to defer a decision for long. This often had unfortunate results. Sure enough, when the muster roll had been filled, a man with better claims and in every way preferable, had to be turned down.

In spite of this inevitably haphazard method of collecting a crew— for it could not be called picking one—on all the Greenland voyages we had been a reasonably happy ship. On a comparatively short voyage of four to five months it is easy enough to:

> Be to their faults a little blind
> And to their virtues ever kind.

And this cut both ways, the crew being prepared to tolerate anything I might do or say seeing that they had not to endure or suffer me for all that long. The crew's ability to get on with each other and to work together is more important than what seamanly qualities they may have. In this respect the enormous crew of ten which had sailed with me in *Patanela* to Heard Island (see *Mostly Mischief*, London, 1966) was remarkable for the absence of friction. But those were picked men, known to each other or to mutual friends, men with like interests and with expedition experience.

My system, if system it could be called, had worked well enough so far. Even if it could be arranged, a short preliminary voyage to try out the crew would have little value. They would be on their best behaviour, zealous and willing to an embarrassing degree, and if one did take a dislike to one of them, a replacement would still have to be found at short notice. Always on past voyages the crews had soon shaped up to their jobs, took whatever was going in the way of food, and made themselves as pleasant as they knew how. I hope I did the same, though no man can be expected to make bright, chatty remarks for five months on end, much less for twelve. It is sometimes difficult to say 'Good-morning' and quite impossible to continue the conver- sation beyond that. Doubts have been expressed as to whether the

Christian virtue of good temper is binding on a man before breakfast. There is a story, quite apocryphal, of a pre-war voyage to India in a P&O liner with a Himalayan climbing party. On reaching the open sea from Tilbury the writer is reputed to have exclaimed, 'H'm, the sea', and on nearing Bombay, after a silence of eighteen days, to have startled his expectant listeners with another profound remark, 'H'm, the land'. But no one goes to sea in a small boat in the hope of leading a social life.

Naturally the finding of a crew for a twelve months' voyage is harder than for one of only five months. Fewer men are able or willing to spare that amount of time. There are therefore fewer from whom to choose. Whether this means that the chances of picking a dud are greater or lesser I am not mathematician enough to say, but the presence of any such will inevitably be that much more difficult to tolerate. For the sort of voyage now in prospect, where conditions would be tough, at times perhaps even daunting, the quality of the crew, their reliability, their devotion to the ship they served and their sense of obligation to finish what they had undertaken to do, became of prime importance. Again, unlike a Greenland voyage, there would be stops in strange, sunny, exciting lands where the temptation to swallow the anchor is strong. Places where:

> Slumber is more sweet than toil, the shore
> Than labour in the deep mid-ocean, wind, and wave, and oar;
> Oh, rest ye brother mariners, we will not wander more.

Besides the attractions of the shore there may be other yachts which, at any rate in port, seem to offer more ease and comfort than hellship *Mischief*, and whose skippers appear to be less of a bastard.

As I say, no special exertions were made to find a crew for this voyage and there was no lack of applicants. Of these many withdrew when they learnt the time involved and our destination, and in the end, as is usually the case, it was touch and go whether we should have a full complement, with no scope left for manoeuvre. In the case of the first few applicants, one is so glad to have any at all that, like the first swallows of summer, they meet with a less critical eye. What unexpected virtues may not lie hidden under that unprepossessing appearance and manner? If this man is turned down, on possibly flimsy grounds, will any more be forthcoming? These are the questions that arise, and one has nothing to go upon but one's own fallible judgement.

Early in 1966 I roped in the first applicant, young Roger Robinson who approached me in person after a lecture I had given at Lymington. He was then at Southampton Technical College taking a course in yard management, and in the happy position apparently of being able to break off and resume after a year's absence. He had had considerable sailing experience, had seen *Mischief* and knew what he was in for, and seemed uncommonly keen. I thought this quality would compensate for lack of size and weight, for he was dimunitive. As Falstaff said: 'Will you tell me, Master Shallow, how to choose a man? Care I for the thews, stature, bulk, and big assemblance of a man? Give me the spirit, Master Shallow.'

Next I had a letter from John Ireland, a stranger, who had heard of me and *Mischief* through a friend of mine in New Zealand. He then came to Wales bringing with him a friend of his, David Shaw. John Ireland hailed from Liverpool (my own home town) and had the Liverpool sound, talking that language so fast that I had always to ask him to repeat what he had said. He had recently done a long trip in a Land Rover, climbing in New Zealand and the Andes on the way, for he was primarily a climber. He had also done some dinghy sailing. The friend, David Shaw, looked the more likely and proved to be just the man I always hope to have with me and so seldom get. I took to him at once; red-haired, sturdy, quiet, and self-reliant. He had been a Conway boy and was then in the Royal Mail Line and had just got his Master's ticket. He had not done much sailing but with his sea background would very soon learn. He would be invaluable to have, both as a competent mate and an experienced navigator, and should we succeed in landing a climbing party on Smith Island he would be able to take charge of *Mischief*. The question was whether he would be granted a year's leave. It would be a bit of a busman's holiday for him but he hankered after a closer familiarity with the sea in its varying moods than can be obtained from a glass-enclosed bridge sixty feet or more above it. Not that there is anything the matter with glass-enclosed bridges. If *Mischief* had to proceed at twenty knots in all weathers one would certainly want to lurk behind glass. On my advice they went down to Lymington to look at *Mischief*, with the result that both wanted to come. It would be some time before David heard about his leave and it was up to me to keep a place open until he had heard.

The first few days down the steamer-infested English Channel with an inexperienced and probably seasick crew can be very wearying, conducive to nightmares and stomach ulcers. On this account alone the presence of a man who has sailed before in *Mischief* and knows the ropes is more than welcome, besides the comfort to be got from having on board from the start a man whom one knows and in whom one has confidence. Nor is this wish to have on board a second-voyager quite so absurd and improbable as may be thought. Not all past crews think that once is enough. Charles Marriott, for instance, has made one long and two short voyages in *Mischief*, thus deserving my gratitude and a medal, too, if I had one to bestow. Roger Tufft was another who had made one long and one short voyage, a man who liked it the hard way, having previously done three years in the Antarctic, subsequently making a crossing of the Greenland ice-cap manhauling a sledge. Bill Procter, too, had taken part in two long voyages when he was of the utmost value to me, having had far more experience. Later he built his own boat, a little twenty-one-foot sloop, in which he had got more than halfway round the world before—alas—coming to grief. In July 1965 he left Guadalcanal for New Guinea, since when no trace of him or his boat has been found.

Setting considerable store, then, on having on board an old hand, I wrote to Bob Cook who had been present on the first, unlucky trip to East Greenland when *Mischief* had been nipped in the ice. I knew he was neither married nor in a job so promising that it could not lightly be thrown up, for he was a long-distance lorry driver. I was glad when he agreed to come. As well as being a climber he was valuable on deck, a big man whose weight on a rope would be worth about three of my more diminutive crew. There remained one place to fill, the hardest to fill in both senses. It is rare to find a man eager to cook at sea, and this is not strange, for dedicated men are rare. *Mischief*'s galley is forward of the mast, the liveliest place in any seaway, and the cooking is done on Primus stoves, primitive, smelly, but safe and reasonably efficient. I have described it elsewhere as 'a role that is exacting and always difficult to fill. A role requiring the balance and agility of a juggler, a strong stomach, and indifference to being alternately sprayed with cold sea water from the galley hatch and boiling water from the stove; the ability to work in a confined space breathing rather foul air, and the energy, patience, and goodwill shown by a hen cormorant in feeding her mouth-gaping offspring.'

A friend of Roger Robinson's, a Swede, volunteered for the job, but owing to the Easter holidays, and his departure for Sweden before he had received my glad acceptance, he managed to escape. A young lad on a motor bike bound for Snowdonia and dressed for the part, a little shaggy withal, then turned up unannounced at Bodowen. Having heard through John Ireland of what was afoot he was on fire to come in the hope of doing some climbing. He had made one or two voyages as a trawler hand and was now learning the trade of welding, two jobs that in my opinion augured well of a prospective cook, the one hinting at a cast-iron stomach and the other familiarity with great heat. Tom O'Shaughnessy hailed from Birmingham and was, of course, Irish, and quick to take offence. His keenness for the adventure overcame his reluctance to cook. We already had two possible climbers but his willingness to cook made me glad to take him.

We were now complete provided David Shaw got leave and I had to put off several possible recruits while this hung in the balance. In mid-July we were due to sail so it was disturbing for me to learn a month before that Bob Cook had fallen off the top of his loaded lorry on to a concrete floor, chipped the bone in both wrists, and would be unable to come. Those whom I now had to fall back on, having previously refused them, were committed to something else or for some reason unable to come. One had taken an Alpine holiday and spent all his money. Time was running out, but having at last heard that David Shaw could come I became reconciled to sailing with five all told instead of six.

At the end of June, just before I left for Lymington to start fitting out, Bob Cook wrote to say that he might be fit enough to come provided he could take things easy for the first few weeks. This welcome news came a fraction too late. Chance governs all. Before I had replied telling Bob to come I had a telephone call from a Mike Edwards, another of John Ireland's acquaintances. He, too, came from Birmingham. 'I have no great hopes of Birmingham', said Mrs Elton, 'there is something dire about the sound of it.' Be that as it may, I should have plumped for Bob Cook, chipped wrists notwithstanding, had not Mike Edwards told me that he was a professional photographer and suggested the possibility of making a film. On two earlier voyages we had made a 16 mm film and I had found the exercise expensive and not repaying. But hope springs eternal in even my breast and I arranged to meet Mike Edwards in Ludlow next morning on my way to Lymington. Besides his photographic background he had sailed racing dinghies and had done his national service in the Navy. True, he had served only as a photographer but he should have learnt something of the sea and the need to keep things shipshape below. As later he showed, he had.

We met in the bar of The Feathers. He was tall, very fair, with a handsome beard of the same hue, a relic presumably of the Navy. Answering a question in the Commons about shark repellants, Churchill began his reply by saying, 'H.M. Government is totally opposed to sharks'; and, stupid prejudice though it no doubt is, I feel totally opposed to young men with beards. However, beard or no beard, I had to decide quickly between these two possibilities and I decided on trying to make a film. This gave Mike barely a week to settle his affairs, collect his kit, find, buy, and have tested a suitable second-hand camera with the necessary equipment. That he managed to do all this and join *Mischief* a couple of days before sailing says much for his energy and ability.

So, for better or for worse, I had my crew, and on paper they looked pretty good. On previous voyages I had sailed with crews of less experience and less promise who had turned out well. How many of this lot were men with whom, according to Monty's well known criterion, one would care to go into the jungle, remained to be seen.

CHAPTER II

TO THE CANARIES

A T THE END OF A VOYAGE *Mischief* is stripped bare. The crew put in two days' hard work carrying ashore the sails, the gear, the accumulated junk of a voyage, unreeving the running rigging, and unshipping and sending ashore all the spars including the bowsprit. The Yard then take out the mast for storage under cover, and the standing rigging, the shrouds and forestays, go into the loft with the rest of the gear. *Mischief* is then taken to her mud berth where she is left to withstand the ravages of winter, no doubt feeling callously neglected. Rot and decay now have the chance to make their insidious attack. To help fight this off a big cowl ventilator is fitted over the hole in the deck normally filled by the mast, and additional ventilators have been let into the foredeck.

Whether the pole mast is the original mast dating back to 1906 is not known. Certainly it is getting on in years and has one or two very long shakes which happily run the right way, up and down the mast instead of across it. These are left open so that no water lodges in them, a plan that is probably better than filling them with stopping material. The mast has practically no taper. An elderly lady, whom I absolve from any rude intentions, once asked me if it had been a telephone pole. Some critics regard the mast, in the words of Mr Chuck the bosun, as precarious and not at all permanent. It is stoutly stayed with two-and-a-half-inch wire, but out of respect for any possible weakness we no longer send aloft the topmast, a heavy spar which extends another twenty feet above the upper cap. The extra weight aloft, as well as the extra windage of its five supporting shrouds and stays, is hardly offset by the ability to set a topsail. Nor in the Atlantic off Iceland and Greenland, where *Mischief* had cruised for the past five summers, would there be many days when a topsail could be carried. Over the years I have become accustomed to her bald-headed look and am not likely to see her fully rigged again until she is reduced to making coastal passages.

All the other spars, boom, gaff, and bowsprit, have been renewed since I bought her in the spring of 1954 at Majorca. The gaff had broken off the Spanish coast when bringing her home in the autumn of that year; the boom broke in 1956 between Bermuda and the Scillies, and the bowsprit broke off Cape Town in 1960. The present boom is a massive affair almost as thick as the mast, strong enough in itself to laugh at the most violent 'Chinese' gybes and heavy enough to smash anything that stands in its way. Even when laying in stately repose on the gallows, its dimensions strike a new crew with awe and dismay; for it is obvious that the least tap from this heavy, blunt instrument would stun the strongest elephant. But, like the threat of nuclear war, its formidable powers are a safeguard and a deterrent. One keeps out of harm's way. So far it has neither killed anyone nor swept them overboard.

Throughout the winter I had been taking home bits and pieces of the running rigging—bowsprit shrouds, backstays, topping lifts, tackles—replacing the wire when necessary, renewing block strops, and overhauling the blocks. In stormy weather, the knowledge that this work has been properly done ensures some peace of mind. On this long voyage south of 21,000 miles, except for a broken sheave in the throat halyard block, nothing in the rigging came adrift. It is not easy nowadays to find old-fashioned wood blocks or the sheaves to go with them, modern yacht blocks being made of anything but wood, diminutive in size as they are high in cost. The main shrouds and forestay are too heavy to be taken home, nor would I care to undertake the job of splicing wire of that size. These are examined by the Yard before the mast is stepped, which is done after the boat has been hauled out for its annual coat of anti-fouling. On this occasion, when towards the end of June the mast was about to be stepped, the shrouds, which had been fitted in 1954, had to be condemned. Under the serving and parcelling of the eyes that go over the masthead, it was found that only a strand or two remained serviceable, the rest being rusted through. Why the mast had remained standing on the voyage home from Greenland the previous autumn is another unsolved mystery of the sea; then, the mast must indeed have been precarious and not at all permanent. This discovery meant a rush job making up new shrouds and forestay, and in order to save time and money—the usual excuse for any unsightliness—I consented to having 'talurit' splices for the lower eyes instead of hand splices. This quick method of swageing wire is reckoned to be as strong or stronger than splicing by hand but it looked out of place in *Mischief*'s old style rigging.

Before this, young Roger and I had started painting below—peak, galley, cabin, and engine-room—a job that must be done before the crew can start living on board. By the time I got down early in July to start fitting out he had about finished the painting. The new shrouds had already been set up but the forestay had been made a foot too long and had to be done again. Pleased though I was to see the new shrouds already up I felt disgusted with myself over the 'talurit' splices which stuck out blatantly, as inappropriate as a tin roof on a tithe barn. Keen-eyed visitors to the old boat commented on their incongruity. They feared that it might be the thin end of the wedge, that before long she would have stainless steel rigging, chromium-plated winches, a metal mast, nylon rope and terylene sails. Such things may be good in the right place, though where that is I would not care to say; but in an old gaff cutter they strike a bizarre note, as if some venerable elder states-man had had himself rigged out in Carnaby Street.

When David Shaw joined we did our best to hoodwink people by serving over the 'talurit' splices with marline. These whims and fan-cies of mine have to be paid for and I suppose this is done through some loss in efficiency. Sails and ropes made from artificial materials, of which new versions are constantly appearing, cost much more but are stronger and more enduring than those made from natural fibres, but the greatest advantage of such sails is their immunity to rot and mildew, so that if need be they can be stowed wet. They have some slight drawbacks. The stitching on such sails stands out proud and is liable to chafe, and bends and hitches taken in ropes of man-made fibres are apt to slip. Personally, I shrink from the noise that some of these new materials make; the flapping of the sails when going about often sounds like small-arms fire. Tom had a windproof smock made from one of these new materials and when he was on deck in a breeze the racket it made was frightening.

By the time the crew began to arrive I had the ratlines made up so that we could get aloft to hang the blocks and reeve the halyards. John Ireland and David limped into the Yard in an ancient and halting car that seemed about to wheeze its last wheeze. John at once advertised its sale. After some hard bargaining it went to a chap in the Yard for £5, the removal of its last seat to add to the amenities of *Mischief*'s cabin having significantly diminished its value. With the arrival of Tom O'Shaughnessy work went on apace, and with everything well in hand David and I spent a day in Southampton for a last shopping round-up and the collection of log books and thermometers from the Meteorological Office. On the Greenland voyages we had recorded observations for the Meteorological Office at Bracknell. Having no transmitter we cannot transmit observations when they are made as is, of course, done by the large fleet of voluntary observing ships.* At the end of the voyage our log books are sent to Bracknell where they are used for analysis. They are of value mainly because the observations, particularly of sea temperatures and ice, are from little-frequented waters. When I wrote to Bracknell about the impending voyage I suggested that the Southern Ocean might lie outside their parish. 'So far from being out of our parish,' was the reply, 'we are very interested indeed in those parts. Since the demise of British whaling we are virtually starved of marine observations from the Southern Ocean. The Royal Research Ships *Shackleton* and *John Biscoe* are our only source of marine data. That is why observations from *Mischief* would be so valuable.'

Mike Edwards having joined two days previously we sailed from Lymington on Friday, July 14th, 1966, bound for the Antarctic by way of the Canaries, Montevideo, and Punta Arenas. A few local friends gathered to see us cast off and on our way down the river the Royal Lymington Yacht Club, according to their friendly custom, gave us a starting gun. Wind of our departure, however, had reached as far as Southampton, so that Southern Television sent a camera team to accompany us out into the Solent where we would hoist sail. As our jib halyard has a perverse habit of twisting I had had the jib made up in stops and when the moment came all the sails went up without

---

*   There are some 500 of these selected ships, covering between them the Seven Seas and representative of the best of the Merchant Navy. The P. & O., for instance, have been recording observations since 1855. In addition there are sixty-five supplementary ships, 108 coasting vessels, thirteen lightships, twenty trawlers, and fifty auxiliary ships whose observations are less full than those of the selected ships.

any hitch. Only the vang, the rope leading down from the peak of the gaff, got adrift. From my position aft in the cockpit I should have secured the lower end of the vang to the boom, but with my eyes on the crew and conscious that the eyes of England, or at least Southern England, were upon me, I failed to grab it in time. Since then I have not met anyone who watched our departure as it appeared on illustrated wireless; anyone who did must have wondered whether the long rope streaming gaily from the peak was *Mischief*'s paying-off pendant. When the television boys arrange to take such pictures they probably think they are doing one a favour, whereas the boot is really on the other foot. The camera team, one hopes, enjoy a nice little outing, and in the course of it, at no cost, obtain the material to fill an otherwise dull programme. The idea of insulting one by offering some payment in return, even to the extent of a coil of rope or a bottle of whisky, never occurs to them.

On a fine, clear morning, the wind at NW force 4–5, we cleared the Needles and headed down Channel. None of the crew except John showed any interest in pilchards for lunch, and unless the sea is unusually calm this is how fresh crews usually react whether or not they have taken anti-seasick pills beforehand. It is a state of affairs that is to be expected and must be allowed for when starting out with an unseasoned crew. It is always a bad thing to have to postpone one's departure but it would be unwise not to do so if really rough weather prevailed. In the Channel where, even in summer, fog or thick weather may develop quite quickly, it is a good thing to know one's position. As soon as we had sunk the coast of England below the horizon I took a sun sight, but before obtaining a reasonable result I found I had to work it several times. Rust is the enemy to combat in maintaining a boat, and a man's brains, after some months ashore, are not immune to its ravages.

At midnight we passed the Casquets and had Les Hanois abeam next morning. Standing away from the French coast we had to reef down in the afternoon, and when the forecast predicted winds of force 6–7 we hove to for the night. The crew were far from well and I wanted to ensure our having some supper. Tom being out of action, Mike gave us a scratch meal of onion soup, cold bully, and spuds. That the forecast proved correct deserves mention, for it is only the mistakes that are usually recorded, often in indignant terms. Conditions were less wild when we started sailing again at 4 a.m., steering WSW with Ushant fifty miles away. Both Tom and Roger remained in prone positions and David was not sure of himself, having to abstain from the cigarettes he delighted in. None of the others smoked. I smoke a pipe and smoke far more tobacco at sea than on land in order to extract the utmost benefit from duty-free tobacco—making hay while the sun shines, so to speak. David, who had never before been sick at sea, felt injured, while I took it as a reflection upon *Mischief*'s sea kindliness, one of her great virtues.

On the Sunday night, a clear night with moderate wind and sea, we raised the Ushant light and by next morning had it abeam with a stream of shipping well inside us. For the skipper at any rate the rounding of this noted seamark had been fairly painless, except that our meals had been a little too simple. On the Monday night, however, Tom made amends by giving us a curry with really dry rice. In the matter of curry I can be a little swinish; it was probably gluttony at supper, and the consequent drowsiness, that led to my having a close shave with a trawler. I had to put the helm hard down to avoid being rammed.

Women who spend much time with horses are said to acquire faces not unlike a horse; in the same way, having spent much time with Sherpas, Tibetans, Khirgiz, Afghans, and such like, I have acquired a taste for hot dishes. These otherwise happy folk never taste meat as we know it in the form of Welsh mutton or Scotch beef. When in luck they may partake of a scraggy goat, a scrawny rooster, or a yak whose diet has been mainly gravel, the kind of meat that needs to be thoroughly disguised even if it means blistering one's mouth in the process. Nor is their liking for fiery food confined to meat dishes. The Sherpas, for instance like all their food spiced; were they to eat anything so anaemic as porridge they would flavour it with chillies rather than sugar. Once, when alone with one in the Assam Himalaya, I made a note of how he doctored his ration of half a mug of pea-soup:

> Taking six large chillies, a dozen cloves of garlic, an ounce of salt, he ground them on a stone to form a thick paste. This was scraped off the stone and dissolved in not more than a quarter cupful of water to which only half the soup was added. Then, with an occasional

shake of the head and a blink of the eyes, the only hint that he was taking a powerful blister and not an emollient like bread and milk, the fragrant mess was quickly hoisted in. The Sherpa likes his sauce piquant.

I was fortunate in once taking a short course in how to eat curries, if not how to make them, in the Western Desert where, in quiet periods, the officers of a Punjabi battalion used to lay on a special curry lunch on Sundays, a rich and gigantic vision of the higher gluttony. The Colonel, a Falstaffian figure in shirt sleeves and shorts, always began by putting a towel round his neck as a sweat rag. Disgusting, no doubt, but highly practical and a mark of respect to the mess cook. Before concluding this dissertation on curry and returning to the Bay of Biscay, I might add that our having curry for breakfast, harmless though it may sound, played some part in the ultimate defection of the crew. On such small things have depended ere now the fate of dynasties. The War of the Austrian Succession, we are told, was ostensibly caused by the loss of his ear by one Jenkins, master mariner, at the hands of the Spaniards.

We made fast time across the Bay with runs of over a hundred miles on four successive days, so that when only six days out we were nearing Cape Villano north of Finisterre. There were the usual tunnymen about, gaily painted craft with tanned steadying sails, their crews hauling in tunny with monotonous ease. This irked us, for we caught nothing on the line that we trolled persistently over the stern; as some wag remarked, we would have no fish on our plate until we got to that river. For a week the crew were kept occupied, if not amused, by scraping the deck. Hitherto the deck had been painted with a mixture of linseed oil and red ochre which looked well and was non-skid. With a painted deck, however, there is a tendency for water to get under the paint and lie there. Our bare deck when wet seemed to me much more slippery and whether with bare feet or in gumboots one had to move with caution. Unlike the single-handed sailor whose time is fully occupied, a large crew in a small boat never has enough to do. Four men could manage *Mischief* comfortably. In her working days, manned by real sailors, two were enough. We had to have six so that if a climbing party were put ashore there would be enough men left to work the

Approaching Neptune's Bellows, Deception Island, on the way out

The Chilean base at Pendulum Cove, Deception Island

boat. We therefore had five watchkeepers, and since in normal weather we keep single watches, a man has a lot more time off duty than on. The few major repair jobs that crop up from day to day are easily handled by one man. On passage, painting and varnishing are not often possible and seldom profitable, while the making of chafing gear such as baggy-wrinkle or fenders, is limited by the amount of old rope on board—usually not a lot. How different from the life of hard labour for the crew of big four-masted sailing ships with their miles of rope and wire and acres of canvas to be maintained, too few men and too much work:

> Six days shalt thou labour, and do all that thou art able,
> And on the seventh—holystone the decks and scrape the cable.

So that apart from watch-keeping and the occasional call to change sails or reef, the crew of a small boat are thrown much upon their own resources—reading, writing, sleeping, or sun-bathing and day-dreaming on deck. In fact, 'stretched on the rack of a too easy chair'.

Having carried us swiftly across the Bay the wind fell light and finally left us becalmed, in fog and in the shipping lane, 30 miles north of the Farilhoes. *Reina del Mar*, a cruise ship, slid by going dead slow, while other ships, to judge by the noise of their engines, were bashing on regardless, some not even sounding their fog-horns. Compared with the strident, threatening blare from a big steamer, the note from our foghorn, blown by mouth, is politely plaintive and of limited range. On some calm foggy day it would be instructive to row off in the dinghy to learn how far its squeak does carry. I suspect that one would not have far to row.

A breeze thinned the fog a little but it did not clear until next day when we found we were twenty miles south of our dead reckoning position. Nothing had been seen or heard of the lighthouse on the Burlings. Whether we had passed between the Farilhoes and the Burlings, or outside both groups, worried David, a most conscientious navigator. Evening star sights were his forte, taking four or even five stars and producing the answer in a very short time in spite of the indifferent cabin lighting. I preferred morning star sights when there was daylight in which to read the tables; even so the results were sometimes less than perfect, the triangle of error that resulted from the plotting, generally known as a 'cocked hat', too often resembled a nine-gallon Stetson. My sextant, made by Bassnett of Liverpool, a firm long defunct, must be pretty venerable. Old shoes, old coats, old friends, are best, but, perhaps, not old sextants. In picking up a star I find it better to discard the telescope, which leads one to suspect that it may be dim with age. However, since the Polynesians navigated successfully with a coconut, price 1 /-, one grudges spending £50 or so on a new sextant. An authority on these matters, though not himself a Polynesian, tells me that celestial navigation by means of coconuts is a myth. But I propose letting it stand. We suffer too much from matter-of-fact people who take pleasure in demolishing our cherished illusions.

The northerly wind off the Portuguese coast soon began to veer east, merging into the north-east Trades which at this time of year are at their farthest north. With 500 miles to go to the Canaries we set the twin staysails and sat back to enjoy an even more leisurely life. Sailing downwind with twin staysails or a square sail brings peace of mind to the skipper and makes for a fast passage. In the latitudes of the Trades the chances of a gale are remote, the gear is free from chafe, and whatever antics the helmsman may be equal to there is no great boom for him to bring crashing over in a 'Chinese' gybe. But like most good things one can get tired of this kind of sailing. The sheets have not to be touched, the helmsman has only to keep the wind on the back of his neck, and the ceaseless rolling becomes a bore. This year the Trade wind seemed less fresh than I remembered on earlier voyages, and since the following seas were not so big the rolling never became so violent as that described on *Mischief*'s first voyage South:

> She seemed to enjoy sailing before a wind that blew true and steady as a bellows, and frequently showed her pleasure by some lively rolling. This rhythmic rolling, inseparable from downwind sailing, becomes a nuisance, particularly at meal times, when a man needs two pairs of hands, or if any work has to be done on deck. Every few minutes the boat would glide gently into a crescendo of rolling, each successive roll becoming livelier and longer, until the dislodging of the helmsman from his seat or a loud crash from the galley, announced that she had had her bit of fun. Then she would sail demurely along until

tempted by the laughing waves to do it again. One could almost hear
her humming to herself:

> Roll me over, in the clover,
> Roll me over, lay me down, and do it again.

By now we were in flying fish waters but only rarely did enough come
on board to provide a breakfast. Flying at night they hit the sails or
some other obstruction (once when steering I was hit in the face by
one), or if the boat is rolling heavily they may be scooped up over the
bulwarks. I attributed the scarcity of flying fish for breakfast to the
fact that we were not rolling enough. Porridge, therefore, or a scramble
of dried eggs, was usually our morning fare. Dried eggs are at their
most exquisite in a cake or a duff where their flavour passes unnoticed
among the more wholesome ingredients. If taken neat they need to be
laced liberally with Tabasco sauce, a sauce that is hot by our feeble
standards, for I doubt if it would blister the skin. Tom had now found
his feet, and—thoroughly mixing the metaphor—began to pull out all
the stops, playing every possible variation within our limited range.
Based firmly for the most part on bully beef, these consisted of stews,
risotto, past'asciuta, dried hash, sausage and mash, and, of course,
curry. As yet my gastronome's diary makes no mention of duffs, the
mariner's prime belly-timber, but they were to come. I read, however,
that we had some difficulty about mashing spuds. 'Have we anything
on board for mashing spuds?' someone asked. 'What size are your feet,
Mike?'

   We were now nearing the Canaries after a pleasant enough passage, but a little worried by the amount of water she was making. The
trouble was traced to a broken cockpit drainpipe. Later in harbour,
when we could plug the outlet with a cork, John put in a length of
polythene tubing. At midnight of July 29th we sighted the Isleta light
on Grand Canary and hove to until daylight before entering the harbour. *Mischief* wears well. Unlike her owner she does not get slower
and slower each year. On the four occasions that she has visited Las
Palmas, from 1955 onwards, she has taken exactly sixteen days from
Lymington.

CHAPTER III

TRAGEDY AT SEA

———◆———

S INCE *MISCHIEF'S* LAST VISIT IN 1959 alterations and extensions have
been made to the harbour of La Luz. Because there were no ocean-
going yachts anchored off it, we ignored what was obviously a new
yacht club and went on to anchor off where the club had been when we
were last here, which was now waste land. We found ourselves among
a thick cluster of local small craft and had not been there five minutes
before a policeman on the nearby wharf told us to clear out. So we
moved to the head of the harbour, an oasis of quiet, as we thought,
until a bucket dredger close by started to work. When no one had
shown any interest or come to clear us I rowed ashore and got a lift
in a truck to the port office on the opposite side of the harbour. It was
open, but only for the sake of a bevy of hostile charwomen who soon
brushed me aside. At last I found the office of the port police where a
chap who sat smoking a cigar, listening to a commentary on a World
Cup match, stamped our passports in between goals. On this Saturday
afternoon no doubt the port authorities in many other countries were
similarly busy. Having made our number at the Yacht Club, where a
swimming gala was in progress, we dined in a cheap joint in La Luz.
Tom had stayed on board and in spite of the racket from the dredger
(which worked all night) heard us when we shouted for the dinghy.

As the dredger seemed unlikely to shift for some time we decided
to move to the Club, having first found that the water off it would be
deep enough. With a view to astonishing the natives we thought we
would sail there and make a running moor. Two natives at least we
astonished, gave them in fact the fright of their lives. What with our
being near the head of the harbour and the wind offshore, the dredger
on one side and a wooden jetty on the other, we had little room in
which to tack. Moreover, *Mischief* was in one of her obstinate moods.
On the first two attempts prudence decided me to bear away at the critical moment. On the third attempt, without doing the fresh thinking

that the situation obviously required, I held on, much to the surprise and dismay of two men in a dinghy fishing close to the wooden jetty. Probably neither could swim, for they stood by their ship like heroes, awaiting our onslaught, without jumping overboard. Our bowsprit cleared the jetty by an inch or so and out of the corner of my eye I could see that the two heroes were still afloat; nevertheless, our manoeuvre, daring though it was, had not been really seamanlike.

Shaken though I was, and indeed the crew as well, no one flinched from the carrying out of the second part of our programme, the running moor. After a couple of dummy runs this went without a hitch. Dashing, in a manner of speaking towards the shore, we turned into the wind, let go the anchor, and had the sails down in a jiffy. Only when a launch full of yachting characters appeared on the scene did we realise that a small buoy close ahead of us marked the finish of a race. Soon the contestants at the end of their eight-mile race hove in sight and our presence close to the finishing mark gave them a last minute chance to display their skill. From the noise made by the excited crews as they were obliged to go about and again about to fetch the mark, one sensed that in their opinion we were in the way. These racing boats were the size of whalers with a big crew and one big lateen sail which demanded smart handling as they went about, loosing the tack, carrying it round the mast, and making fast again at the stem.

Several launches with spectators were in at the finish and presently one of them came alongside. A thin, grey-haired man in a battered black velour asked in excellent English if if he could do anything for us. Gravino, as he was called, proved an invaluable ally during the rest of our stay, bargaining with shopkeepers, arranging for stores and water, and dealing with officials. Among us only John had a smattering of Spanish, having spent some months in Montevideo on his world tour. Gravino, a widower, lived alone with a pet dog in an ancient fishing boat moored in the harbour. He had been a fisherman and gave us much unavailing advice on how to catch fish; his English had been learnt while at an American base during the war. He made heavy inroads on our whisky, though protesting his dislike of it, his favourite tipple being Bacardi rum and coke. He was seventy odd, and when we remarked on his agility and fitness he told us, much as a man might boast of doing twenty 'press-ups' before breakfast, that he daily drank sixty-five small glasses of rum and coke. The night before we sailed we joined him at his favourite bar, his home-ground so to speak, where he scored a century not-out.

No one from the Yacht Club paid us a visit; perhaps we looked too much like a working boat. A big French ketch came in for a couple of days and later a Fairmile launch from Durban. The latter must have had a foul time bucking the north-east Trades; an ocean voyage in a small power boat is my idea of hell, it must demand from the crew uncommon endurance. The short stay made by these two and the absence of any other yachts contrasted strongly with the dozen or so that had been present on our earlier visits, yachts that had been manned mostly by what I call seagoing beachcombers who were in no hurry to move. Most of them—American, Canadian, Australian, German—had been bound for the West Indies and were awaiting the passing of the hurricane season. Others might be waiting the arrival of funds, or waiting there to earn funds, or merely waiting, Micawber-like, for something to turn up. I remember vividly a small weather-worn sloop lying next to us, whose owner, a bearded German, old enough to have known better, had with him as partner or crew a sort of Gypsy Queen, all flashing eyes and teeth. While he went shopping with a string bag the Gypsy Queen, or Princess Pocahontas as I called her, sat on deck ogling *Mischief*'s crew. There may be fewer cruising yachts at Las Palmas but a vastly increased number of fishing vessels now use the harbour, small trawlers of many nationalities but mainly Japanese. In recent years the waters off the African coast opposite the Canaries have proved to be one of the world's richest fishing grounds.

Except for Tom who was short of cash the crew spent their days ashore and seemed fully occupied. Mike, in particular, as was his way in every port, gave the impression of being rushed off his feet, a man working against time, writing notes, and taking the name and address of everyone he met. But they were all models of decorum, unlike the crew of 1957 who on arrival had disappeared to a man, returning for breakfast the worse for wear, one of them having been robbed of all he possessed. We made a point of meeting about 11 p.m. at the Club jetty in order to avoid someone having to turn out later in the night to fetch off belated arrivals. The descent into the dinghy down a long, iron ladder presented no difficulty but one night David, who was cold sober, missed the dinghy. His anger on being fished out of the water was so evident that our natural impulse to laugh had to be quickly suppressed. His smart, shore-going rig had all to be rinsed out in fresh water.

On August 6th we went alongside the fish wharf to take in water. If we were to fetch Montevideo at one hop as intended we needed all the water we could carry and a bit more. The main tank in the cabin, on top of which is our table, holds a hundred gallons; a deck tank holds another forty gallons; and there is another side tank in the cabin holding thirty gallons. Besides this there is a five-gallon iron-bound water-breaker lashed on deck, which many people think ought to be full of brandy, and a few smaller containers. Altogether we can carry about 180 gallons which, at three gallons a day, would allow us to be at sea for sixty days. This would not be enough and we relied upon collecting thirty to forty gallons of rain water in the doldrums, an expectation that in my short experience has never failed. The water is in charge of the cook and no one gets any to drink except in the form of tea, coffee, or cocoa. The washing of either body or clothes is, of course, out, except with sea water. Shaving water is allowable but only Tom and I availed ourselves of this. While watering I went with Gravino to collect our clearance papers. On the way back a fisherman friend of Gravino's presented me with a fish, a big, red, Roman-nosed brute whose coarse looks belied its fine quality.

Having paid Gravino for his services with a bottle of the whisky he despised and drank so heartily, we sailed out. We were well stocked with provisions and one or two of our containers had in them something better than water. As the Spaniards say, a day without wine is a day without sun, and at all our ports of call as far south as Punta Arenas wine is to be had good and cheap. It had been a moot point whether we should take our departure for the South Shetlands from the Falkland Islands or from Punta Arenas, and the fact that we should be able to stock up with wine there may have tipped the scale in favour of Punta Arenas. We took a large quantity of twice-baked bread, 'tostada', which is merely sliced bread or rolls put in the oven and toasted. In less than ten days bread is usually too mouldy to be eaten even by the least fastidious while 'tostada' seems to keep indefinitely. We had no less than three sacks full.

Having obtained a good offing to clear the southern end of Grand Canary we set the twins and let her go. The Trades blow pretty fresh in the vicinity of the Canaries. Leaving Las Palmas bound south is like stepping on to a train; for one can hoist the twins secure in the knowledge that for the next 800 miles one will drive steadily on course logging over one hundred miles a day. That afternoon the wind increased to force 6 or 7. In one watch we logged six knots and in the next seven knots, just about as fast as *Mischief* can be expected to go without coming apart at the seams. Chased by the following seas she yawed about a lot, so that until the wind moderated after midnight we had two men on watch. The point was that the helmsman in order to call his relief has to leave the tiller for a minute or two to nip down to the cabin, and under the twins she does not hold her course nearly so steadily as under fore and aft rig, no matter how cunningly the tiller is lashed. With no one at the helm to correct it, a violent yaw might fetch one of the sails aback. On one occasion some genius at the helm brought off the almost impossible feat of getting both the twin staysails aback. My metaphorical train on to which we had stepped when leaving Las Palmas proved to be a stopping train. After a run of 520 miles in five days, on the next day we did only twenty-five miles. Whether he is concerned with the erratic behaviour of a storm or the ordered regularity of the Trade winds, a seaman counts on nothing from the weather except its power to surprise him. As Captain MacWhirr remarked of the Laws of Storms: 'All these rules for dodging breezes and circumventing the winds of Heaven, Mr Jukes, seem to me the maddest thing.' Still, the Trade winds at least ought to conform to the rules; their northern or southern limits shift and may exceed or fall short of the accepted average, but a sudden failure of them at their very heart gives good reason for surprise. On the night before this sudden lull—though it cannot be cited as cause and effect—we had admired a dazzling display of phosphorescence during which a school of dolphins struck streaks of fire as they crossed and recrossed the ship's glowing wake. For two days the wind picked up again enabling us to score runs of 108 and ninety miles. The rougher sea brought on board some flying fish and for the first time we had enough for breakfast. In my opinion they are as good as fresh herrings. I see, too, from my gastronomic notes, that Tom had mastered the technique of duff making. The gannets among us, which was our term for the gluttons, had barely finished breakfast before they were speculating on what the day might bring forth, that is to say, the size, shape, flavour and richness of the evening's duff—like those men of whom Dr Johnson speaks, 'whose principal enjoyment is their dinner and who see the sun rise with no other hope than that they shall fill their belly before it sets.'

On the 14th the wind failed again and as we lay becalmed that evening—though nothing could be seen—we reckoned we were only a few miles north of Boa Vista, the easternmost island of the Cape Verde group in Lat. 16 N. These islands are supposed to lie within the belt of the north-east Trades throughout the year. The sailing ship track passes to the west of the islands, where it is possible we might have had steadier winds. But I wanted to sight the islands, or at least to let the crew see them, in particular the island of Fogo and its 9000-foot volcanic cone of which on an earlier voyage we had enjoyed a spectacular glimpse. Islands, ships, whales, marine monsters of any kind, birds, even bits of seaweed, all arouse the keenest interest and break the tedium of a long ocean passage. They form subjects for argument and give the crew something to talk about other than the shortcomings of the skipper. Alas! We saw nothing. For us the Cape Verde Islands might not have existed, for the haze that so often prevails in their vicinity in summer had reduced visibility to less than two miles.

On account of this, the indefinite horizon, as well as the unreliability of a meridian sight, the sun being now almost overhead, we were uncertain of our position—an uncertainty that could not but cause anxiety in view of what the *Admiralty Pilot* has to say of this region:

Chart 366 should be used with great caution, especially in the vicinity of Boa Vista, off which many uncharted dangers exist. The haze over the whole group is often so thick that the surf is sighted before the land. The eastern islands more especially feel the force of the south-westerly set and several wrecks have been caused by disregarding it. It is recommended to give the east coast of Boa Vista a berth of at least 7 miles.

Admiralty Pilots necessarily abound with gloomy remarks of this kind, painting the worst possible picture, so that the mariner who comes unstuck cannot say he has not been warned. Therefore, upon hearing what I took to be the noise of breakers, at the first breath of wind we stood away to the south-east.

> Beyond the clouds, beyond the waves that roar,
> There may indeed, or may not be, a shore.

The crew suggested the noise was that of a jet plane warming up, but I could see no possible connection between jet planes and an island like Boa Vista, and this mythical jet continued warming itself up so long as we remained in earshot. By the following evening, when a west wind had cleared away the haze, we were too far south to see any of the islands.

The sights that we did at last obtain put us twenty miles south of our dead reckoning. We were having difficulty in getting time signals and at this juncture David managed to put the chronometer watch back in its case upside down, thus effectively stopping it. This watch had been purchased ten years before, secondhand for £5, and on only one voyage, when the mainspring broke, has it stopped. It has a steady rate, generally gaining two or three seconds a day when the temperature increases, and losing again by a similar amount in colder regions. For news and time signals we carry a Decca transistor receiving set, and normally an aerial inside the cabin suffices for picking up the BBC Overseas service in any ocean. Now, in order to make sure of receiving a time signal, we rigged an outside aerial, and having got one we were able next night to restart the chronometer.

During the next few days the wind varied greatly in strength, one evening a flat calm and in the succeeding night enough wind to split the genoa. During the evening calm, the weather bright and sunny, we piped all hands to bathe and skylark. Skylarking was the word, ducking each other, diving from the rigging, belly flops and bottom flops. And for supper we had what we called a cheese flop followed by a jam sponge. Flop consisted of potatoes, cheese, and onions churned together and baked. At last on August 19th, in Lat. 8° N., we had the rain we expected and needed. With a roll in the mainsail water trickles off briskly to be collected in saucepans and buckets hitched at various points along the boom. Later we rigged the canvas skylight cover under the boom like a canvas bath. A watering party, stripped naked, stands by to empty the saucepans and buckets into the deck tank. The single roll that we had put in the mainsail for collecting water soon had to be increased on account of wind, the prelude to a black, wet, thoroughly unpleasant night. This bout of rain lasted for twenty-four hours.

The wind now settled down at south or a point or two either side of it, the very direction in which we hoped to steer. Whichever tack we sailed on, owing to leeway, we could make but little to the south, perhaps ten, or at the most twenty miles of southing as a result of twenty-four hours sailing. Why worry, one might ask, South America lies to the west so why not steer west? The snag is that a ship which fails to cross the Equator far enough to the east is set to the west in the grip of the Equatorial current at the rate of twenty miles a day until it finds itself hard up against the coast of Brazil. In the days of sail a square-rigged ship that found itself unable to weather Cape San Roque at the north-east corner of South America might have to fetch a circuit of the North Atlantic in order to try again. One is well advised not to go on the port tack to start steering west until south of Lat. 40° N.

Notwithstanding, our reluctance to sail in the opposite direction to our destination overcame reason. For the next two or three days we steered stubbornly westwards on the port tack, always hoping that the southerly wind would free us by hauling more to the east. In fresh winds and a moderately rough sea we were going west at the rate of eighty miles a day and very little to the south; and it was in these unsatisfactory conditions that a most unexpected and inexplicable tragedy overtook us. Coming on deck at 07.40 on August 27th, I found the ship on course, the helm lashed, and no sign of the helmsman. It was hard to believe but it did not take long to satisfy myself that David, who had the watch from 06.00 to 08.00, was not on board. After a hasty look in the peak, the galley, and the cabin I gave the alarm, turned out all hands, and gave the order to gybe. In a few minutes we were sailing back ENE on a reciprocal course with all hands up the shrouds scanning. The sea flecked with white horses, dark cloud shadows moving slowly across it, the sea that for the last few weeks we had sailed over so care-free and unthinkingly, had suddenly assumed a pitiless aspect.

We soon noticed that the patent log had stopped rotating and on hauling in the line we found that this had broken about two-thirds of its length from the counter. It is by no means unusual to lose a rotator; on the present voyage we lost two. Either it is bitten off by a shark or a porpoise, or the line frays at the point where it is attached to the rotator. But the line is less likely to break or be bitten through at any other point, accordingly we assumed that it had broken when David grabbed at it, or even later on when his weight on it had combined with a sudden lift and snatch of the counter to put too much strain on the line. The entry in the logbook by the man whom David had relieved at 06.00 was 1830 miles and the log had stopped recording at 1831. In short, we concluded that if the line broke when David grabbed at it, as seemed most probable, this must have happened about 06.15, so that he had already been overboard for an hour and three-quarters. My heart sank. In so far as we were not shipping any water on deck the sea could not be called rough, but for a man swimming it was far too rough. I did not see how a man unsupported by a lifebelt could long survive.

Assuming the worst I decided to sail back a full seven miles, which in theory would take us to the ship's position at 06.15, the time at which the accident had probably occurred. After that we could start searching back across our track. I say 'in theory' because it could be only the roughest guess-work. How much leeway would she make? Would it be the same that she had made on the opposite tack? Would the speeds be the same? Even an error of a half-point would in the course of seven miles bring us to a position that differed by nearly one mile. And in the conditions prevailing, the white horses and the increasing glare of the sun on the water, we should be lucky to spot a man's head even three or four hundred yards away. When so much depended, or might depend, upon the course we steered, upon our making a lucky guess, my feelings as I sat watching the compass may be easily imagined.

By 10.00, when we had run our distance and sighted nothing, we handed the sails, started the engine, and began to motor back across our track, ranging about a half-mile either side of it. A sound enough plan if we were approximately in the right place, otherwise perfectly futile. Nor could one suppress the terrible feeling that we might have already sailed past David, that he had watched *Mischief*'s familiar mast go by and that we had failed to spot him. The crew continued their watch from up the shrouds where they remained throughout that most dismal day, one of them in turn coming down for a bite of food. Standing on the ratlines, hanging on to the shrouds hour after hour, taxed both strength and determination. With no sails to steady her *Mischief* rolled and pitched heartily and the higher a man is above the deck the more violently is he flung about. For the first two or three hours hope buoyed us up but as the weary day dragged on we became increasingly despondent; until at last the lengthening hours since the first news of the disaster finally extinguished hope. A small school of dolphins chose this day of all days to accompany *Mischief*, leaping out of the water and turning somersaults with a gay abandon that contrasted bitterly with our despairing gloom.

At 18.30, the sun about to set, I decided that no more could be done. Setting main and staysail, we hoisted a riding light and hove to for the night, unwilling to leave the scene of the tragedy and uncertain of what course to steer. Were we to continue to South America or turn for home? It seemed best to sleep on it. In the morning I could ask the crew what they wanted to do. Apart from all its other sad aspects, the loss of David Shaw was a wellnigh fatal blow to my hopes and expectations. As mate, as a competent navigator, a reliable, likeable man with whom I could get on, a man whose training imbued him with a sense of loyalty to the ship in which he served, his loss was irreparable. None of the others had the knowledge, the experience, or the force of character needed to take his place. With no one now who could take charge of the ship in my absence, Smith Island at any rate was out of the question. Had I known what might happen, as by then I should have guessed, I need not have waited to consult the crew before turning for home.

Although it has no bearing on the present case, I thought that to end this chapter, a brief account of a 'man overboard' incident that had a miraculously happy ending, might be of interest; an account for which I am indebted to my friend Commander Erroll Bruce.

In 1951 during the trans-Pacific race to Honolulu a man fell overboard from the yacht *L'Apache*, just before breakfast in broad daylight, the weather clear, wind and sea moderate. A white lifebuoy was

immediately thrown to him. The yacht was running with every possible sail set and with a spider's web of preventers, downhauls, and
stays rigged to keep the sails full. In these circumstances half an hour
elapsed before the yacht was under control and able to steer towards
the scene of the accident. But in that comparatively short time those
on board had lost their position relative to the man and they never
found him. Meantime the man, who was not wearing oilskins, had got
inside the lifebuoy which was fitted with an automatic light. By daylight, however, the light was useless, and by nightfall its battery had
run down.

An American naval fleet that happened to be exercising in the
vicinity intercepted distress signals from *L'Apache*. A widespread search
with destroyers and aircraft began. Several of these passed close to and
were seen by the man sitting in the lifebuoy, but it was not until next
day, in a final sweep before the search was abandoned, that he was
sighted and safely picked up.

As Erroll Bruce points out, the vital thing in such circumstances,
when for some reason a boat cannot immediately be turned, is to keep
the man in sight or to know how his position bears relative to the boat.
As well as the lifebuoy for the man himself, anything that floats should
be thrown overboard at intervals as markers for the track on which to
sail back.

CHAPTER IV

ARRIVAL AT MONTEVIDEO

T HIS ACCIDENT, SO OBSCURE, so unexpected, and so unnecessary, hit us hard. For the first day or two one could not realise that it had actually happened, that there was not some mistake, and that David was not merely absent from the cabin on watch and would presently come below. An accident calls for some explanation and it is the more disturbing when no reasonable explanation is forthcoming. We discussed it at length that night and on subsequent occasions without any useful result. David had kept the meteorological logbook and 06.00 was one of the times when observations were made. When taking the sea temperature he had what I thought the bad habit of leaning out under the guard rail to lower the thermometer into the sea, instead of drawing a bucketful of seawater. As *Mischief*'s freeboard amidships is less than three feet this was easy to do. That he might have been doing this and had leant out too far occurred to me at once, but when we found both thermometers on board in their usual place this possibility had to be ruled out.

Again, the vang, its lower end clove-hitched round the outer end of the boom, sometimes comes adrift and has to be recaptured, usually by a man leaning out over the rail with a boathook. I have had occasion to do this and have then stood on the bulwarks at the counter (where, by the way, the guard rail ends) to refasten it round the boom. I have done this when no one else was on deck to see me fall in, or likely to come on deck for some time, which goes to show how careless or over-confident one can be. But, as we could see, the vang was fast nor could we find anything loose in the rigging or adrift on deck to account for David having lashed the tiller and left it. That it had been so securely lashed that *Mischief* had held her course for so long was another puzzle, though I knew that David enjoyed playing with the tiller and so adjusting things that *Mischief* sailed herself. How fatally successful he had been! If the helmsman leaves the tiller to put

55

something right on deck he would normally take a few turns round it
with the tiller line and a couple of hitches. This would be good enough
for the few minutes before the line worked loose, the tiller shifted, and
the boat came up into the wind. Even when on the wind *Mischief* does
not sail herself for long and I was astonished that on this occasion she
had held her course for nearly two hours. If only David had not been
so successful in lashing the tiller! She would soon have flown up into
the wind, when the ensuing racket, the flapping of sails and banging
of the boom, would inevitably have woken and brought me on deck
to see what was happening. In which case we should have had more
chance of saving David.

That night it rained heavily, a sure sign that we were still in the
region of the south-west Monsoon and not yet near the south-east
Trades. In fact our dodging about on the previous day and heaving to
at night had probably lost us more ground to the north. In the morning, much to my surprise, not one of the crew expressed any desire to
turn back, a desire to which I would have been ready, even glad, to
accede. In fact I felt like turning back and had opinions been divided
would have done so. But to insist upon turning back seemed unfair
because it would have been easier for me than for them to give up the
voyage and arrive home unexpectedly. True, my arrangements for a
year's absence had been made, but had I returned I should not have
had to start looking for a job, as they would, or in some cases for lodg-
ings. Nor would it be for me, as it might be for them, the only chance
of making a long voyage to strange lands.

So we decided to proceed, though I made it clear, or thought I had
made it clear, that there could be no attempt to land on Smith Island.
On the other hand we were a quite strong enough crew to take the boat
to the South Shetlands, even though morale had been a little shaken.
And for my part, without David to back me, there would be more work
and worry. We agreed to remain on two-hour single watches, and in
order to prevent the four watchkeepers having always the same watch
Tom volunteered to take the afternoon watch. As a meagre compensa-
tion for cooking, the cook had all night in and could afford to miss the
afternoon siesta when most of us liked to get our heads down. 'Sleep
that knits up the ravell'd sleeve of care,' or what the sailor vulgarly
calls a good kip, is probably more valued by seamen than by anyone

Mischief anchored off the Chilean base, Pendulum Cove, Deception Island

because their sleep is usually brief and often broken. A thoroughgoing seaman can sleep at any hour in any circumstances. For my part daylight sleeping is hard to come by except in the afternoon, and the more welcome therefore I found Tom's assurance of always having the afternoon siesta, however sordid one usually feels after this indulgence.

A noon sight for latitude (Lat. 05° 15′ N.) showed that we had been set north as I had feared and that in the three days that we had been on the port tack we had made little or no southing. We therefore went back to the starboard tack steering ESE, determined to remain on it until in Lat. 40° N. Wet and windy conditions continued until September 1st, when the weather brightened and the light, fleecy clouds sailing overhead had all the appearance of a Trade-wind sky. We began to steer towards our destination instead of away from it, and as a bonus we collected no less than eight flying fish from the scuppers. Dorado, too, were seen in numbers, those big, brilliantly-coloured, swift-darting fish, sometimes confusingly called dolphins, a fish that when caught makes a dish fit for Lucullus. When caught! Alas! Our lures were tried in vain, whether bright bits of tin, white rags, or red rags, all were alike ignored or bitten off.

Just as the full moon excites lunatics and makes wolves howl, at sea it gives me the itch to take star sights. The stars are so much easier to see than at dusk or dawn, and since the horizon appears to have a razor-edge sharpness it seems a sin to ignore such perfect conditions. On one such calm, velvety moonlit night I took a sight of Fomalhaut at 1.30 a.m. when it happened to be on the meridian, and on working it out found that we ourselves were exactly on the Equator. The result may well have been a mile or so out but when the sum of latitude came to precisely o degrees it gave me peculiar pleasure. Indeed, such pleasure that I thought of rousing out the crew to share it. There is, as the Bible tells us, a time to keep silence, and a time to speak, and on the whole, 1.30 a.m. is the time for silence.

The value of star sights by moonlight is debatable. So great an authority as Lecky, author of Lecky's *Wrinkles*, has no doubts on the matter and is willing even to dispense with the moon: 'A man of ordinary vision, using a good star telescope and well silvered sextant glasses, will find little difficulty at any time on a clear night (especially if the moon be up) in obtaining all he may want in the way of reliable sights.' Commander Cobb, on the other hand, the editor of a modern edition of Lecky, is not so sure:

> We all know that the moon possesses a 'mysterious influence', that moonlight plays many tricks of fancy. One of these tricks may well be to present to the mariner a false horizon, be the latter's appearance ever so sharply defined. Nevertheless, stars have been and will continue to be observed on a moon horizon, but such sights are not recommended and should always be treated as suspect.

To offset this warning the Commander goes on to quote the interesting case of the grounding of a cruiser on Quelpart Island off Korea early in the century:

> The navigator, in default of any better means of ascertaining his position, had been able to obtain a hurried latitude by Polaris in moonlight. This latitude placed him some ten miles to the northward of his dead reckoning, a state of affairs which he considered to be highly improbable. His horizon had been uncertain; he therefore ignored the observation, despite the fact that he was approaching the island from southward. Alas! At the court-martial which inevitably followed, it was discovered that his latitude by Polaris was more accurate than that of his dead reckoning. The moral here is an old one—if a choice of positions presents itself, always consider the ship to be in the position of greatest danger.

No question of danger arose in our case, for we were still a good 2000 miles from Cape Polonio where we hoped to make our landfall. All this moonlight navigation or, as some might say, moonlight madness, was of merely academic interest. Nevertheless the South Equatorial current was setting us west at such an astonishing rate—on one day a difference of forty miles between the course steered and the course made good—that at times we seemed more likely to make a landfall on Cape Recife, at the north-east corner of Brazil, than on Cape Polonio 1500 miles to the south. After crossing the Equator we took advantage of a calm sea and a moderate breeze to launch the dinghy and embark a camera party to take pictures of *Mischief* under sail. Mike Edwards had the 16 mm. cine camera and with him went John Ireland festooned with all the cameras on board, while we sailed off down wind preparatory to making several runs close past the dinghy.

The wind began to haul more easterly, as it should further south, but it also blew harder than one expects in the SE Trades. In ten days we logged 1130 miles, hard on the wind for most of the time, a point of sailing which makes *Mischief* creak and groan. She also leaks more than one cares for when sailing hard, especially in way of the chain plates and around the stemhead. Leaks at least keep the bilges sweet and exercise the pumps. We have an old-fashioned barrel pump worked from on deck near the cockpit with a minimum of effort and with satisfactory results, and another, a most efficient 'Whale' pump, mounted in the heads. In view of the serious nature, as I thought, of the voyage I had it fitted in place of a rotary pump which demanded a lot of effort and had a nasty trick of siphoning back. We even had a third pump but as it had been carried for years without being used this had rusted solid. In Montevideo I passed it on to a mechanically minded boat-owner on condition that he removed it. This had been worked, or should have been worked, off the charging engine, an imperfectly reliable source of power, as engines must be. 'It is but machinery, Sahib,' was the excuse offered to me by an Indian truck driver when his truck broke down. The theory behind the fitting of this expensive, work-saving appliance was that after days of gales, *Mischief* half full of water, the crew would be too exhausted to work the pumps, but in such conditions, I think, the charging engine itself would have been the first thing to have its spirit quenched by the quantity of water on board. In order to save a few minutes' hard labour there is a tendency nowadays to waste money on mechanical devices that at an inopportune moment may let one down.

Meantime the over-fresh winds obliged Tom and I to put in a lot of palm and needle work maintaining the genoas. We had two of these big sails. One had already done several voyages and was not expected to last long, while the other, a second-hand sail bought for the voyage, had turned out to be a thoroughly bad buy. 'Flapping Fanny', as we called the latter, was not robust enough to start with and soon wore itself out, the leech flapping incessantly even when running. Having wasted much time and sail twine on it we stripped off the hanks, bolt rope, and cringles, and threw it over the side. It had lasted just long enough for Tom and I to patch a tear of twenty feet or more in the older sail.

The dorado that now began to haunt the ship and our inability to catch them drove us well-nigh frantic. They lived under the hull in perfect peace and amity with scores of lesser fry, the whole aquarium menaced only by man, their common and not very deadly enemy. Neither by fair means or foul could we kill one. John Ireland managed to lodge a harpoon in one which wriggled off just before we had got it on board, while Roger lost another which he had foul-hooked when jigging a bare hook over the side. At the same time we lost another rotator but I doubt if a dorado had tried to make a meal of that.

Having run through the SE Trades we entered the region of variable winds. Variable indeed! After a prolonged run under The Twins before a northerly wind, we had to drop them in the middle of the night for a sudden shift of wind to the south accompanied by a deluge of rain. The rain came in useful. By now, forty-five days out, we were well into the main tank and had just lost two gallons by upsetting a container in the galley. The southerly wind and sea increased all day until after being hit an awful crack when a sea leapt on board we decided to heave to. At first I feared that this sea had broken the skylight. In rough weather we rig a canvas cover over the skylight, but even so jets of water force their way through. As my bunk has no upper berth above, it is the more vulnerable and frequently gets soused. All ills are good that are attended by food, says the philosopher, and that night, being Sunday night, we had curry and a treacle duff, a pudding fit for a glass case. Maybe the rough weather had affected the appetites of the crew. So much curry remained uneaten that I told Tom to dish it up for breakfast. Like Mrs Gilpin, though on pleasure bent, I have a frugal mind.

That human life is everywhere a state where much is to be endured and little to be enjoyed was a thought that had not yet penetrated the minds of the crew. John in particular, a great traveller by his own account, had not learnt that a traveller should have the back of an ass to bear all, and the mouth of a hog to eat what is set before him. The curry, appearing at an unusual hour, was still hot enough to inflame him. On this occasion I caught his drift quick enough when he

violently voiced his disgust at being expected to eat curry for breakfast. This chap who had eagerly volunteered to come on this voyage,
who would have been disappointed had he been refused, who was now
enjoying a free holiday, had apparently persuaded himself that he was
doing me a favour. It is a question whether those who contribute nothing towards the expenses of a voyage have any right to complain, if
they do complain it needs to be done tactfully.

Running parallel with the coast of South America, now about
sixty miles away, we began sighting ships. Nowadays the sailing ship
route to South America is so lonely that one can safely forget about
navigation lights. Until one begins to close the land the sighting of a
steamer would be a rare and memorable event. Nor is there much life of
any kind in this watery desert, the North and South Atlantic on either
side of the Equator, where the sighting of even a bird almost warrants
calling those below. Perhaps one might see the odd storm petrel, the
smallest and commonest of all ocean birds, ranging from the Southern
Ocean to the North Atlantic. More rarely, always aloft and never on
the water, one might see the lovely and highly predatory frigate bird
with its long forked tail; or perhaps a bosun bird with an even longer
tail, the bosun's marline spike. As far north as Lat. 20° S. we saw the
first albatross, the yellow-nosed albatross which is found much further
north than the big wanderers. Cape pigeons, too, sometimes gathered
round the boat, and these pintado petrel are one of the commonest
birds of colder southern waters and the most attractive. Owing to their
chequered black and white plumage, they have the rare merit of being
easily identified by the most myopic bird-watcher.

Having been at sea for fifty days, and with less than a thousand
miles to go, we all felt the passage had lasted long enough. It had so
far been fairly fast for *Mischief*, and had we not unnecessarily covered
three or four hundred extra miles through going on the starboard tack
when too far north of the Equator, we should have been even quicker.
The twice-baked bread, fresh to the very last, had now given out and
we went on to biscuit. With Primus stoves, the baking of bread for a
crew of six would consume too much time and paraffin to be feasible.
The 'Lifeboat' biscuits we use are small, tasty, and not too hard; they
serve so well for conveying to the mouth large quantities of butter and
jam that they have to be rationed. Our porridge, too, ran out, and this

at least had the advantage that we used less water for cooking. The small amount of paraffin we had left gave me more concern. After four consecutive days of light winds when we did less than fifty miles a day, I decided to reduce our consumption by cutting out the mid-morning tea or coffee—our 'elevenses'. The crew took this hard, blaming me, quite rightly, for not buying enough paraffin. However, when we had done three runs of over 120 miles a day everyone cheered up. At sea there is nothing like swift progress for keeping tempers sweet.

Overnight on October 2nd the sea temperature dropped from 67° to 60° F., indicating that we had crossed what is called the sub-tropical convergence... upon which my early morning bucket baths became less frequent. On some voyages these early morning showers had been carried to extreme lengths, or extreme north and south latitudes, an unspoken but well understood challenge between one or two of us leading to a contest of obstinate politeness as to who would be first to quit. A 'sudestada', a moderate southeasterly gale accompanied by heavy rain, sent us scurrying along under close reefed main and jib throughout a murky night. By morning it had cleared and that evening we sighted land fine on the bow and about fifteen miles distant. By midnight, drifting with all the sails down, we had Cape Polonio abeam.

Motoring through thick fog on a windless morning we presently came up with a small fishing boat engaged in long-lining. In exchange for cigarettes they gave us dog fish, edible enough in spite of their name. Small rockhopper penguins were bobbing out of the water, and what appeared at first sight to be wreckage or floating branches turned out to be seals sleeping on their backs with their flippers in the air. They breed on the island of Lobos at the entrance to the Plate estuary, which we passed about a mile off at 3 a.m. of a wonderfully bright, moonlit night, the seals and penguins making noises according to their kind, barking and braying. As the day advanced the breeze on our quarter freshened so that we finished this long passage with a flourish, romping through the dirty, yellow water of the River Plate at a good five knots. As we passed Flores Island near Montevideo the wind grew fresher raising a short, choppy sea. Puerto Buceo, a small fishing port and the headquarters of the Yacht Club, is about nine miles east of Montevideo. It was too insignificant to appear on our chart and my memories of the place were faint.

Closing the land in search of it we had trouble in making out any landmarks at all owing to haze and the glare of the westering sun. Despairing of finding it I was about to make for Montevideo harbour when we spotted the breakwater and the nine-storey club building. Off the entrance the water is shallow and each time we dropped into a hollow between the steep waves I felt sure that *Mischief*'s keel would hit the sandy bottom. All went well and we anchored in a most undesirable berth in only one-and-a-half fathoms of water, the fishing boats inside the breakwater and the yachts lying off the Club leaving us little choice. Nor was that the worst. When the anchor went down we found that Mike Edwards, intoxicated by the city lights, had omitted to put the chain through the fairlead. Not wishing to have the bulwarks chewed to pieces by winching up the cable, we hauled all forty-five fathoms of it up from the locker, passed the bitter end back through the fairlead and restowed. Tom, who is not loquacious, thought this an occasion that called for remark. He had served in trawlers, so he gave Mike, and us, a fairly close idea of what the eloquence of a trawler hand would have been in like circumstances. We were sixty days out from Las Palmas, having sailed 5300 miles.

CHAPTER V

TROUBLE AT MONTEVIDEO

A T A BRITISH PORT a yacht flying a 'Q' flag would probably be boarded by the Customs and Immigration officers in a matter of hours. At Puerto Buceo we lay for weeks unvisited, and only when we showed signs of leaving did the authorities sit up and take notice. On our first visit here in 1955 things had been different, but then we had gone to the main harbour where we unwittingly drew and promptly received attention from a whole posse of officials by anchoring in the fairway for the arrival and departure of seaplanes. Their present unconcern seemed the more surprising because there is a water-guard in permanent session in a room on the ground floor of the Clubhouse where several policemen, in pseudo naval uniform, sleep, eat, smoke, and drink maté tea, their job being to keep an eye on visiting yachts. These rare visitors are mainly Argentine yachts on a week-end sail from Buenos Aires a hundred miles away up the river.

Ignoring the police, and ignored by them, we all went ashore the morning after our arrival to take a bus into the city. A member of the Club from whom we enquired about bus routes pressed upon us an ample sum of Uruguayan money to pay our fares. The first essential was to report the presumed death of David Shaw to the British consul who would no doubt find means of informing his parents in England. At all costs I wanted to avoid their first learning of this through the newspapers, and for that reason I intended saying nothing to the Uruguayan authorities. From them the local press would probably have got wind of it and the news would not be confined to Montevideo. Accidents to yachtsmen or climbers are meat and drink to the British press to whom the news would undoubtedly be passed. In the crew list I had made out for the Port authorities, expecting them to show some interest in us, I had omitted David Shaw's name. Subsequently this led to a bit of bother.

It took about half an hour to reach the city by bus, the fare then being 2½ pesos or about 6d. When we returned in the spring of 1967 the fare had doubled. In the course of the next three weeks I made this journey so many times that it became wearisome. Its distance from the city is one disadvantage of Puerto Buceo, but on no account should a visiting yacht lie in the main harbour. 'There be land-rats and water-rats, land-thieves and water-thieves', and Montevideo abounds in both. They operate on a wholesale scale. We heard of one steamer that had had fifty 5-gallon drums of paint removed from her deck in the course of a night.

Nowadays journeys by land are more perilous than sea voyages. This bus ride had its hazards. The buses have three doors, front, middle, and rear, operated by the driver. On some you enter by the rear door and leave by the front or middle, on others this order is reversed. A comparatively bucolic customer like myself found it puzzling. On one occasion, having put a hand inside the middle door, the wrong one, preparatory to entering, the door closed and the bus moved off. Had it been the left hand (we drive on the right in Uruguay) I might have sprinted alongside to the next stop, but with the right hand jammed in the door I was facing the wrong way and had to start running backwards. Fortunately a passer-by, who had less contempt for gringos than the bus driver, persuaded the driver to stop before he had gone far. It would be charitable to think the driver had not seen me, but more probable that he wished to teach the gringo to use the right door.

Now that we had arrived events moved quickly and trouble came thick and fast. Only later, when Tom and I were alone together, the sole survivors of the crew of six which had left Lymington with such high hopes, did I learn what had been brewing for some time. Had I known I might have been more circumspect. As the Swahili say: 'Cross the river before you start reviling the crocodile's mother.' John Ireland I expected would leave and his loss was no great matter: even if we got no one else the four of us could have managed. Apart from curry for breakfast he had some complaints about our fitness for the voyage. A bolt securing the gaff saddle to the gaff was worn, the sheet winches slipped, as, too, did the anchor winch. As a matter of personal interest I let the offending bolt remain and it was still there when we returned to Lymington. With a full crew sheet winches are a luxury on a cruising yacht; in any case, if it is blowing hard and the sheets need hardening the boat can be run off or brought to the wind. The links of the chain did not exactly fit the cogs of the anchor winch so that a link or two occasionally slipped back. Short of a new cable or a new winch, patience and a foot pressed hard on the chain are the remedy.

His real grievance was that we had no distress signals and carried no life-raft. In my view every herring should hang by its own tail. Anyone venturing into unfrequented and possibly dangerous waters does so with his eyes open, should be willing to depend on his own exertions, and should neither expect nor ask for help. Nor would equipment of this sort be of much use in Drake Passage where the chances of being picked up are so slim as to be hardly worth considering. A yacht is supposed to carry distress signals but is not overmuch reliance placed upon them by owners of small craft? A man with a boat that may be in many respects unseaworthy will happily put to sea secure in the knowledge that at least he has his distress flares. Yearly around our coasts so many calls are made upon the various rescue organisations that by now the average man should be ashamed to think of adding to their number. The confidence that is placed, and successfully placed, in being rescued fosters carelessness or even foolishness, and condones ignorance. More care and thought might be taken if there were a penalty for the firing of distress signals, say £25 a flare, the proceeds to be collected by the R.N.L.I., the fine to be remitted only if proof were forthcoming that the boat had started out in all respects seaworthy and had been in real danger. The perils of the sea are less apparent than the perils of climbing and have to be carefully assessed. In climbing the penalty for a mistake is obvious and is sometimes exacted instantaneously, so that on the whole there are fewer foolish climbers than foolish amateur sailors.

But to return to John Ireland with whom I now parted company, feeling that he and I would not get on together however many life-rafts we carried. To my surprise and chagrin Mike Edwards, with whom I thought I had got on tolerably well, then announced that he would go too, and forthwith they both packed their gear and went. If possible this show-down should have been postponed until we had reached the South Shetlands where there would be neither the opportunity nor the temptation to leave the ship. One regretted the unfortunate proximity of the Yacht Club where rooms could be had comparatively cheaply, where there were all the attractions of gracious living and convivial company. The defection of the older men could not but affect young Roger who, though he professed to be still game, was obviously in two minds about it. He seemed to be waiting for an excuse to book a room at the Yacht Club—if he had not already done so—and the opportunity soon came.

As I have said we were in a poor anchorage. The water was so shallow that at times we were sitting on the bottom. The tidal rise and fall is only a few feet and the depth of water at Buceo depends more upon the wind, a strong blow from anywhere between SE and SW having the effect of raising the level considerably. What with the shallowness and the little scope we had to swing, we had very little chain out. Two days later a hard wind from SW soon showed how insecure we were. We began to drag and to drag fast, fortunately in broad daylight.

Close astern of us lay an eight-metre yacht which some months before had sunk at her moorings where her owner seemed quite happy to leave her, and where she had become part of the scene, a natural hazard, as it were. Before our engine could be started we had slid past this wreck and I fully expected that our anchor, which Tom and Roger were struggling to get up, would foul it. By some miracle it came clear and having got it in we steered for the breakwater, now swept continuously by waves, in order to secure alongside a fishing boat. Owing to the strength of the wind, and the difficulty I had in steering and seeing to the engine throttle at the same time—I almost ran our bowsprit through the remaining rigging of the wreck. Imagination boggles—at least mine did—at the thought of a sunk yacht with another securely fastened on top of it. After this shambles, when we were finally made fast alongside the fishing boat, Roger instantly repaired to the Club, to take advice as he put it, and presently returned to announce his departure. He had lost confidence, he said, we were too short-handed, without life-raft or flares, sheet winches slipping, anchor winch slipping etc.

Tom, who remained steadfast and extremely cheerful at this crisis in our affairs, told me that he had fully expected something of the sort. For the last few weeks of the passage the three malcontents had been discussing their course of action on arrival at Montevideo. Our own course of action now needed discussing. There are over a million people in Montevideo and it would be strange, I thought, if we could not find two or even three enterprising enough to sail southwards with us. By now we had come so far that to turn back hardly bore contemplation, the time for that had been when we were still north of the Equator. So having done what needed doing in the way of maintenance I made almost daily journeys to the city calling at the consulates and shipping offices, particularly the German and Scandinavian. Though sympathetic none of them knew of any likely candidates. The most obvious recruiting ground, the Yacht Club, was also the least likely to provide anyone. Apart from dinghy racing one suspects that their sailing is done in the bar. The Club had very kindly given us the run of its facilities, and very useful they were, but none of the members were sufficiently interested to pay *Mischief* a visit. Perhaps they had heard all they wanted to know from our late crew who were now resident members, but the main barrier was probably language. Surprisingly few spoke English.

The British consul required from each of the crew a written statement concerning the loss of David Shaw and did not think that there would be any need for an official enquiry. The news of his death had been sent to his parents through the Foreign Office and soon appeared in the British press whence it rebounded. Soon the news appeared in the Montevideo papers and we had visits from Reuters' agent and from the Daily Express man at Buenos Aires asking for more details. Meantime the search for crew had drawn blank. Even Punta Arenas looked far away and the South Shetlands right off our map. Tom and I discussed the idea of the two of us sailing to Cape Town, shorter and easier than the voyage homewards. Tom would get some climbing and a crew to take the boat home would have been easily found. By then the season would have been too far advanced for going south, and in any case, owing to contrary winds, it would be impossible to sail to the South Shetlands from Cape Town. For two men in *Mischief* it would have been a hard voyage.

The onward march of progress has inevitably extinguished a few trades and professions—chimney-sweeps for instance, body-snatchers, crimps. At Montevideo I regretted that there were no longer any

Iceberg in Bransfield Strait, between South Shetland Islands and Graham Land

Sea elephant at Grytviken, South Georgia

crimps, men dedicated to making more widely known the benefits of a seafaring life. Two or three bodies delivered on board, drunk or doped, might have cost money but would have saved time; they would have been as useful as those we eventually got and might have been less of a nuisance. In the absence of crimps, or of resorts like Smokey Joe's or Big Nellie's, I had in the end to apply to the Sailor's Home run by the Salvation Army.

The home did not cater only for sailors, all were welcome. Most of the inmates were perhaps men who had had losses and deserved them, modern examples of Falstaff's ragged company, 'revolted tapsters and ostlers trade-fallen; the cankers of a calm world and a long peace.' The Home lay near the docks and its cleanliness inside contrasted with the dirtiness of the street outside, for the Major in charge, an Australian, saw to it that his lodgers earned their keep. Montevideo, by the way, struck me as having become a little unkempt. The standard of living had gone down, too. One never saw what had been a common thing on our visit in 1955, workmen sitting round a fire on the pavement broiling two-inch-inch steaks for their lunch.

In a short time the Major found three men for me to interview. They were anxious to get to Europe, to Germany for preference, were willing to work their passage, and did not shrink from the idea of going there by way of the South Shetlands. One of them who had no trade, no skills, no experience, and not a word of English, I thought better to discard forthwith. The second Uruguayan was quite black, looking like a more refined negro. The majority of Uruguayans are European in appearance and this chap, Carreo Javiel may have had his origin in Brazil. Mixed crews in small boats, like mixed marriages, need thinking about. We are all as God made us, some of us much worse, and no one can help his colour. Racial integration is a subject much to the fore and I felt sure that Tom, who hailed from Birmingham, would assimilate or stomach a black crew as easily as I could. Besides we could not afford to be choosy and this man Carreo had one skill which we needed. He was a marine engineer, having served as such in the Uruguayan navy, from which he had a discharge book alleging him to be of good character. He was intelligent and had a fair smattering of English. As it would take a little time to get used to the idea of living with him at close quarters, I deferred my decision. But Carreo was more

than anxious to come and determined not to be put off. For several successive nights after supper we would be hailed by a lanky figure on the
breakwater requiring to be brought on board. Having him on board
for a cup of tea and a cigarette was good practice for Tom and I in the
matter of racial integration. He certainly had a noticeable smell and
no doubt he thought the same of Tom and I and *Mischief*'s cabin. His
anxiety to please and his persistence wore down my instinctive resistance. I agreed to take him—no pay, find his own gear, and a passage to
Europe by way of the South Shetlands and Cape Town. His geography
may have been a bit scattered but he must have understood our general direction and we impressed upon him that the climate would not
be like that of Montevideo. I could see that Carreo meant business and
that he would undoubtedly be with us on sailing day.

The last of the trio was a young German, Herbert Bittner, aged
about thirty, fair, slim, nimble and active—physically the makings of
a sailor but, as we were to learn, totally lacking in any sea-sense or
the ability to acquire it. His life history was obscure and his habit of
romancing added to the obscurity. Apparently he had been in Montevideo about six months and in that short time had gained some noto-
riety. Many people had heard of him or of the incident in which he
had rather mysteriously figured. According to his account he had been
found lying on the steps of a church, having been knocked on the head
and robbed, and instead of the aid and comfort which he naturally
had expected he had enjoyed a short spell in the 'calaboos'. Some said
he was a Jew, in South America on the track of Nazi war criminals,
and that this knock on the head had been by way of a hint to lay off.
About one period of his life there was less doubt. He had once been a
racing cyclist and at the slightest provocation he would produce his
most treasured possession, a packet of press cuttings in which the great
Bittner hit the headlines—pictures of him and his bike, Bittner and
his silver cups, or Bittner being garlanded in Delhi. He was extremely
plausible and self-confident—'no problema' was his favourite expression—and assured me that he had had some sea experience and could
cook, the experience having been gained on a voyage to India in his
father's yacht. Well, he may have had a father, but the yacht, I am
sure, was as imaginary as his sea experience. He had, however, the
great merit of cheerfulness, chattered a lot, and was amusing in small

doses. He spoke a little peculiar English and enough Spanish to help us out with Carreo whom, of course, he knew as a fellow lodger. I had a word with the German consul. In his opinion Bittner was mad and that anyone thinking of going to sea with him could not be quite sane. For all that he would be extremely grateful to anyone who took him back to Germany as he, the consul, could then close the Bittner file. Certainly Herbert was what might be called excitable and perhaps that tap on the head had done nothing to calm him. My friend the Major spoke well of both of them, eager to have them taken off his hands. But there is less in this than meets the eye, as Tallulah Bankhead used to say. Neither of them had given him trouble, only as a good Salvation Army man he would naturally be delighted to see any of his down-at-heel, out-of-luck lodgers shifting for themselves, or at least eager to do something rather than hang around the Sailor's Home. So I decided to include Herbert Bittner in our growingly assorted company. If he proved equal to taking over the galley, as I hoped, Tom could be more usefully employed on deck.

We had been in Montevideo over a fortnight, and now had a crew of four, when the unexpected happened. Our three deserters had made themselves at home in the Club where they might be seen taking their mid-morning coffee on the terrace whence they could keep an eye on *Mischief*. Like two countries whose hostility towards each other has reached the point of severing diplomatic relations, my only contact with them, if contact were needed, was through a third party. One day Tom, the third party, told me that Mike Edwards would like to come back. He was evidently one who acted on impulse; his having left seemed as unreasonable as his wish to come back. His desertion had no doubt influenced young Roger with the result that I had been obliged to take on two questionable characters. Still, if only for the sake of continuing the film that he had begun I welcomed this news and after a brief talk he decided to rejoin. Bygones were to be bygones. For all that he took care not to do any work or to return on board until the day we sailed. As I am writing of real people and not fictitious characters it will not do to impute motives. Why Mike thought fit to rejoin is nearly as beyond conjecture as what song the Sirens sang. It is even possible that he thought, as most people would think, that the least to be expected from a man who volunteers to crew is that he sees the voyage through even when things turn out to be less agreeable than he anticipated.

No sooner had we thus increased our crew to five when along came a young Argentinian and a friend. The Argentinian had just started life in the merchant service and hankered after more experience, while his Uruguayan friend was studying medicine. They were far better types than my two from the Sailor's Home, but I could not take both and the one would not go without the other. We would therefore have to sail with only five. The plan was to go to Punta Arenas and make a final decision there according to how the crew shaped. Either we could continue southwards, or spend some time in, say, Beagle Channel, where Tom and I could climb something, or at the worst head straight for Cape Town. The latter would be the quickest way home. I had friends to see there, and *Mischief* could be hauled out for a scrub at the hospitable Royal Cape Yacht Club. That was the general idea, but I knew that having arrived at Punta Arenas, with the South Shetlands just the other side of Drake Passage, I would be extremely reluctant to abandon our original aim:

> ... But something ere the end,
> Some work of noble note may yet be done.

So we began to get ready. Carreo and Herbert came to live on board and the necessary stores were delivered. Carreo, eager to please, cleaned and repainted the engine and made a thorough job of it. I had to wait for some money from home and we had still to take in water. All the Montevideo Banks were on strike, mere chaos reigned, all correspondence, including my credit note, lay unopened. Buying stores proved far more expensive than I had bargained for and I regretted having spent £10 on yet another rotator for the log, a second-hand one at that. When we first streamed this, by the way, we found it to be an Irishman's rotator, going widdershins, against the sun. Nowhere in Montevideo could we find a *Nautical Almanac* for 1967 and I had little hope of finding one at Punta Arenas. Twice-toasted bread, 'tostada', was another important item that we had to go without.

One of the shallower parts of Puerto Buceo is off the Club quay where we had to go for watering. A steady SW wind piles up the water and one evening, having taken a sounding and consulted the

Club bosun, I thought we had a chance of getting near enough. Since the anchor-dragging debacle we had been lying to a buoy which had become vacant, so we had therefore no anchor to heave in. This was just as well because Tom had gone ashore and only Carreo and Herbert were there to help. We managed to approach within thirty feet of the quay, which was as near as we dared go, and ran a hose on board, a hose that provided such a meagre trickle that we looked like being there all night. While busy attending to this I was peremptorily ordered on shore by one of the police, evidently alerted by our preparations for departure. They were extremely annoyed at my failure to report to them the loss of David Shaw and there were complications arising out of the changes that had taken place since our arrival. Before anything else I must provide a certified copy in Spanish of the relevant log entry lodged with the British consul.

We finished watering as darkness fell. Much to my surprise we were still afloat, the water holding up well, and by now Tom was back on board, slightly drunk and in uncommonly high spirits, responding to every order with hearty, seamanlike Ay, Ayes. We had not room to turn *Mischief* round—she needs a lot of room—so the passage back had to be made stern first in the dark, a short voyage but one pregnant with disaster. When going backwards one never knows how *Mischief* will react to the rudder, the propeller being offset on the port side; whether it will have the normal reverse effect, the opposite effect, or no effect at all. Strictly speaking we should have hoisted two red lights to show that we were not under control. To assist in this manoeuvre and to pick up the buoy, I had one half-drunk Irishman and two aliens, one of whom did not understand what I said, while the other may have understood but did not know what to do. But *Mischief* behaved like a witch. With the tiller steady amidships she described what mathematicians call a Cartesian oval, a beautiful curve which took us safely round the head of a jetty, past innumerable yachts, and to the vicinity of the buoy. With more hearty Ay, Ayes Tom, armed with a torch, went off in the dinghy and to my relief at once found the buoy.

One day when the bank opened for a few hours, while the senior members of the staff who had no reason to be on strike, dealt with their angrier customers, I collected my travellers cheques. But the police were being awkward and refused to give us a 'salida' or clearance. An old friend, Mr McClew, of Maclean and Stapledon, an old established firm of shipping agents with whom we had dealt in 1955, came to the rescue. His years of experience in dealing with officials had not been wasted and his *suaviter in modo* approach seldom failed. We hurried back to the ship, collecting Mike on the way. Having put Mr McClew ashore we were just hoisting the dinghy in when the police launch came alongside to tell us the port was closed. In gale or near gale conditions Puerto Buceo is closed to yachts and fishing vessels, and its closure is signalled by a red flag. We could have got out safely but in view of our recent relations with the police it was wiser to conform. The police wanted to take away our clearance papers to ensure that we did conform, a request that we quickly refused.

CHAPTER VI

TO PUNTA ARENAS

W E SAILED NEXT DAY, October 28th. The distance to Punta Arenas is not much more than 1200 miles; that we had to sail nearly 1700 miles and took twenty-eight days to do it shows how fickle and contrary were the winds. Calms, light airs, and fogs, broken by an occasional short-lived gale, were our portion. In 1955 on this passage we had managed to average only fifty-six miles a day. Such conditions are unlooked for since one is traversing the Forties and Fifties, from Lat. 35° S. to Lat. 55° S., where one might expect to be pushed along by strong westerlies for most of the way. As well as fast, this passage should also be smooth because with the Argentine coast lying all along the weather side the sea has no great fetch. It is probably the effect of the land, too, that makes the Westerlies off this coast so comparatively feeble.

At sea with a fresh crew the wind for the first few days can hardly be too light, and a number of quiet nights without any alarms made up for our lack of progress. By dint of drifting, motoring, and a little sailing we crossed the 120-mile-wide estuary and started down the Argentine coast. According to our £10 Irishman's rotator we were going backwards and to remedy this we pasted over the face of the patent log a new clock face that read anti-clockwise, if that is possible. As we had only four watchkeepers we each did a four-hour watch in the morning instead of the usual two-hour watch. Herbert performed in the galley according to his lights but could eat nothing himself in spite of the flat sea. The most that could be said of our meals at this period was that they had the merit of the unexpected. On one unmemorable evening, having finished our prunes and rice, we sat for some time awaiting the arrival of a non-existent main dish, on the false assumption that Herbert had got the courses back to front.

But he surprised and delighted us by catching two fish and an albatross, one of a flock of twenty or so which had swiftly gathered round us, as we lay becalmed, to fight for the fish offal. These were of the species known as the 'Shy albatross' and their behaviour belied their name. Nothing could drive them away. We ate the fish and put the albatross back in the sea. In the days of sail the catching of alba-tross with line and hook was common practice despite the widespread belief that to kill an albatross is to ask for trouble. It seems that in those days the price obtained for albatross skins, especially in Austral-ian ports, effectively overcame any superstitious feelings the sailors may have had. Birds quickly increased in numbers and kind—Magel-lan penguins, albatross of several species including the wanderer, giant petrels, prions, Cape pigeons, and the ubiquitous storm petrel.

One evening when we were south of Mar del Plata in Lat. 40° S. we fell in with a fleet of Russian trawlers. We sighted the first of them as we ran fast to the south-west under the twins having already logged 143 miles, by far the best day's run of the passage. Alarmed by a fall in the barometer from 1025 mbs to 1010 mbs, we then put a reef in the twins. But no evil came and need not have been feared for the barometer was merely returning to normal after having been abnormally high. Later, when the wind suddenly backed to west it brought with it a blast off the land that felt like superheated air. Whereupon it fell calm and we lay there for the rest of the night surrounded by the lights of fifteen Russian trawlers. Our nearest neighbour turned a searchlight on us and could only be persuaded to turn it off when I signalled by lamp the letters BYM, or Bon Voyage.

With a morning breeze we continued on our way. Soon the father and mother of the fleet, a big factory ship also fitted with a stern trawl, closed us and steamed along on a parallel course less than fifty yards away. Her skipper spoke a rude sort of English and we had quite a long 'gam'. Then they switched on a loud-speaker and played Beatles records for us, or so Mike interpreted the hideous din. As is the way with Russian ships there were a number of women on board, floosies, or in this case perhaps fishwives, to whom our crew made the appro-priate grimaces and gestures. Whether these were interpreted as com-radely or lascivious it would be hard to say. Herbert, besides being a bit of a comedian, never wasted an opportunity. When he waved aloft a frying pan the Russians at once took the hint and threw overboard a parcel of fish with a buoy attached. So we drew away and hauled round to pick it up. To my shame the two attempts we made to grab it were unsuccessful. With the genoa up and a freshening wind, manoeuvring became difficult. Twice we came up into the wind over the buoy and each time we drifted back before it could be grabbed with the boathook.

Between them the Russians and the Japanese have led the way in discovering new fishing grounds. For more than a hundred miles off the Argentine coast the depth is less than a hundred fathoms and further south the continental shelf grows wider until in Lat. 51° S. it extends to the Falkland Islands, over 300 miles from the mainland. If there are fish there this constitutes a vast trawling ground.

This pleasant episode had been marred only by my bungling of 'catching' the fish, and it cheered us on a cheerless, grey day. On the blackest of black nights, with a rising wind, Carreo had the watch till midnight. Generally I tried to keep awake when he was on watch, but this time the banging of the boom and the slatting of sails woke me up. He had got her in stays, the whole mainsail proving too much for him and the boat. A man who has never before sailed a boat cannot learn to steer in a matter of days, but Carreo never learnt and owing to our inability to communicate we could not teach him. Nor did he much care for being taught anything. He knew the points of the compass; that is to say, if you told him to steer, say, south by west, and indicated the point with your finger, he would stick to it regardless. If the wind shifted so that the boat stopped sailing, well, so much the worse for the wind.

Perhaps to keep the crew amused and their minds off the sea we were following the coast at no great distance. Usually I like to get well away from the land; as Conrad rightly observed, 'the true peace of God begins at any spot a thousand miles from the nearest land.' The following night I had hoped to pick up the Punta Delgada light, but at dusk the weather thickened so we altered course away from the land. For supper Herbert gave us fried spuds, and cabbage with custard, a meal that together with the fog filled me with gloom and foreboding. We stole along very quietly over a smooth sea, the silence broken only by the ripple of water along the hull or the melancholy mooing of a penguin, seeing nothing but the guard rail three feet away and the light of the stern lamp reflected in the fog. I had the impression that we had somehow got into a landlocked gulf where imaginary currents were sweeping us on shore. Joy cometh with the morning. By 05.00 the fog had cleared and I got some star sights.

As the sun rose higher the wind died away to nothing. The hardier among us basked on deck stripped, the air temperature being 65° F. and the sea 55° F. Presently a halo formed round the sun, the glass had been falling, and a low bank of cloud or fog to the south-east put me in mind of what had happened in 1955 when a like bank of cloud had advanced upon us before a wind which in a matter of minutes had risen to gale force. This time the cloud heralded nothing more than a hard breeze which by nightfall began to moderate. Another exasperatingly calm day followed and yet another windy night. At the witching hour of 02.00 Mike treated us to an imperial 'Chinese' gybe, the boom flying over with an almighty crash carrying all before it. Nothing had broken, but rather than lie awake below waiting anxiously for an encore I decided to heave to until daylight.

Having sighted land at its northern end we ran fast across the 120-mile-wide Gulf San Jorge in weather more like what it should be in Lat. 47° S. We were still running fast close-reefed when we sighted the land on the southern side of the gulf and a lighthouse which we took to be that on Penguin Island. In my *South American Pilot* this was described as a circular iron tower painted in red and white bands, and the slight discrepancy between what we saw and what we should have seen we ascribed to bad light, bad paint, or possibly my out-of-date *Pilot*. Penguin Island awoke memories of John Davis, the Elizabethan seaman-explorer whose tracks in Greenland waters I had sometimes tried to follow. In 1591 he, too, had deserted northern waters and had gone south in company with Thomas Cavendish. This side of Magellan Straits they were separated and Davis, after persistent attempts to pass the Straits, was finally driven back. He put into Port Desire near Penguin Island to refit for the voyage home. As the name implies penguins were to be had in some quantity. They killed and dried 14,000 which for an estimated voyage of six months allowed a daily ration of five penguins for four men. The voyage home did take six months but long ere this their stock of imperfectly dried penguins had gone rotten. The stores, the ship, the men themselves, became infested with maggots—'There was nothing', wrote John Jane, one of the crew, 'they did not devour, only iron excepted'. When the noisome worm-ridden *Desire* at last struggled into Bearhaven in June 1593 only sixteen of her crew remained alive and of those only five were able to stand.

Later that night we raised the Cape Guardian light thirty miles to the south, a light that we were fated to see again. Another of those curious blasts of hot air off the land heralded a south-westerly gale throughout which the glass steadily rose. By dawn we were hove-to close reefed, and before breakfast we rolled down the mainsail even more. Despite the lively conditions Herbert produced porridge for breakfast, his swan song. All complained of his cooking and Mike had some hard things to say about the state of the galley—saucepans containing remnants of food growing a crop of mould, bits of bread and rotting potatoes stuffed away in odd corners, the stoves coated with congealed fat and bits of rice and macaroni. A deplorable mess that would have made a soft-hearted sanitary inspector weep. In my opinion it does not do to be too fussy about the milieu in which food is cooked so long as the final product answers expectations, but in Herbert's case it did not. Anyone accustomed to native cooks, using 'native' as a convenient label for the black, brown, or yellow inhabitants of wherever it might be, knew better than to intrude upon the kitchen which was probably a grass hut with an earth floor and an open fire.

Mike generously offered to take over the galley where he soon had things shipshape. But we had other troubles on our hands. Herbert who had been unwell from the start now had toothache and talked of retiring to hospital at Punta Arenas. Carreo, so zealous and resolute before we sailed, also talked of leaving; one day because he could not have three hot meals a day, and the next because Tom had sworn at him. We were aware that defection on the part of either of these two new recruits would put in jeopardy the continuation of the voyage southwards. Carreo we decided, must be kept sweet, more difficult though this became every day. He was extremely touchy, so that anything said to him that he did not immediately understand, and that applied to most of what we said, he took to be an insult.

The gale took off by the following evening, but this southwesterly blow, together with a north-going current, had set us back about thirty-five miles to the north-east. A day later, when we were again becalmed, we once more sighted Cape Guardian. For the next week we averaged only some thirty miles a day. In the Roaring Forties, as in other notoriously windy regions, placid conditions may often prevail. It is much like giving a dog a bad name. Off Cape Horn, or the Cape of Good Hope, the so-called Cape of Storms, or in the Roaring Forties, though the yachtsman may expect to be blown out of the water it is a comfort to know that such forebodings are not always fulfilled.

The generally light winds had a mean habit of piping up at night. At midnight on a night of howling wind and driving rain we sighted the San Julian light; by 8 a.m., when we had it abeam, the wind dropped to a gentle breeze. Herbert, who had been promoted to the deck, had the afternoon watch, and while we were all asleep took the boat within a few hundred yards of the beach. With him, as with Carreo, a given course became a fixed idea, something to be adhered to even if it meant taking the boat overland. San Julian, one hundred miles to the south of Port Desire, is where first Magellan, and then Drake sixty years later, both stayed for some time in order to refit and to nip in the bud incipient mutinies; where Magellan hung two of the leading trouble-makers and marooned two others, one of them a priest; and where Drake had John Doughty beheaded. Drake's subsequent exhortation to his followers is well known:

> For I must have the gentlemen to haul and draw with the mariners, and the mariners with the gentlemen; and let us show ourselves to be all of a company, and let us not give occasion to the enemy to rejoice at our decay and overthrow. I would know him that would refuse to set his hand to a rope; but I trust there is not any such here.

Once more we closed the land near the sonorously named San Francisco de Paula, remarkable for its three- or four-hundred-feet-high white cliffs. Though having a resemblance to the white cliffs of Dover these are not of chalk but of clay and gravel. By this we had left the Forties for the Fifties and still the winds remained light and inconstant. Our consecutive runs of twenty-five, twenty-five, eighty-four, seventeen, forty-eight, and six miles show the pattern of the weather. At sea in sail patience is very necessary, but as Dr Johnson remarked patience is a virtue easily fatigued by exercise. As crews often do under such slow progress, we were all becoming a little irritable in spite of the vast improvement in our fare that Mike had wrought. Even Carreo con-descended to eat and to approve his curries. In the important matter of duffs his use of Quaker oats instead of flour marked, I believe, a revolutionary break-through in the field of marine duff-making, and resulted withal in some masterpieces of angelic lightness. Pudding is perhaps too coarse a word for the sort of thing that should be eaten on bended knees.

By the evening of November 20th we were by dead reckoning about eight miles east of Cape Virgins at the entrance to Magellan Straits. We had run our distance so we hove to in thick fog with a force 6 wind at north. Uncertain of our position, and not daring to let draw, we drifted slowly to the south-east all next day in the same dismal fog. A seam in the mainsail opened and part of the leech rope came adrift, so we changed it for the trysail while Tom and I put in a long, cold spell stitching. Next day the fog cleared and in the evening we sighted a great flame of natural gas from an oil well near Cape Nombre on Tierra del Fuego. We had drifted some thirty miles south of Cape Vir-gins and had to work back north to enter the Straits. The number of oil wells both on the mainland to the north of the Straits and on Tierra del Fuego has increased greatly in recent years. Many of them are marked on the chart and where there is also one of these perpetual flames they are readily identified and make valuable landmarks.

Punta Arenas lies about 120 miles inside the Straits and the naviga-tion of this eastern section involves the passage through the First and Second Narrows where the tidal streams run strongly—five to eight knots at springs in the First Narrows and slightly less in the Second Nar-rows. A small vessel must therefore work the tides. An important factor is that the west-going stream, the flood, begins to run three hours before high water by the shore and continues running for three hours after, the reason being that the tidal range outside the Narrows is forty-two feet while inside it is only half that. Thus the water level outside has to rise twenty-one feet before it can begin its rush through the Narrows.

On the 23rd, the wind being light, we resorted to the engine. After puzzling my head over this tidal conundrum I reckoned that with the help of the engine we should arrive within striking distance of the First Narrows in time to catch the evening tide. When still some eight miles away we picked up a strong northerly wind, cut the engine, hoisted sail, and went along at a rare bat, the flood tide having begun to run. I made a mess of the approach and the current swept us to the south side of the entrance where we had some anxious moments on the edge of the Orange Bank in a patch of turbulent water. In the Narrows, which are about two miles wide and ten miles long, there are alarming looking eddies and whirlpools hinting at submerged rocks, but the strait is in fact deep and free from dangers. Shooting out of the Narrows, the flood still running, we made for the northern shore where we anchored for the night. We lay wide open to the west, whence all the weather makes, so we set an anchor watch.

When we weighed anchor at 5 a.m. to catch the tide for the Second Narrows and so to Punta Arenas the same day, we were soon baffled by head winds. Giving up the unequal struggle we squared away and came to anchor off the north shore in Gregory Bay a cable's length from the beach. Waiting for the tide to turn we spent the day there, watching trucks passing along the road which now links the numerous oil rigs to the east with Punta Arenas. Alas! A hundred years ago, when these coasts were really wild and strange, we might have spent the day parleying with Patagonian Indians. The *Beagle* on her famous voyage anchored in Gregory Bay and Darwin thus describes their stay:

Came to an anchor in St Gregory Bay. On shore there were the Toldos of a large tribe of Patagonian Indians. Went on shore with the captain and met with a kind of reception. These Indians have such constant communication with the sealers that they are half-civilized; they talk a good deal of Spanish and some English. Their appearance is rather wild. They are clothed in large mantles of the guanaco (a deer) and their long hair streams about their faces. They are much painted, many with their whole faces red, others black. One man was ringed and dotted with white like a Fuegian. The average height appeared to be more than six feet; the horses who carried these large men were small and ill-fitted for their work. When we returned to the boat a great number of Indians got in; it was a tedious and difficult operation to clear the boat. The captain promised to take three on board and everyone seemed determined to be one of them. At last we reached the ship with our three guests who had tea and behaved quite like gentlemen, used a knife and fork and helped themselves

with a spoon. Nothing was so much relished as sugar. They felt the
motion and were therefore landed. A large party went on shore next
day to barter for mantles etc. The whole population of the Toldos
were arranged on a bank having with them guanaco skins, ostrich
feathers, etc. The first demand was for fire-arms, and of course, not
giving them these, tobacco was the next; indeed, axes, knives, etc.
were of no esteem in comparison to tobacco. It was an amusing scene
and it was impossible not to like these misnamed giants, they were so
thoroughly good-humoured and unsuspecting.

Unhappily, and quite naturally, the last of Darwin's good-humoured
giants has long since been extinguished. As Mark Twain said: 'Soap
and education are not so sudden as a massacre but they are equally
deadly in the long run.' The captain with whom Darwin had gone
ashore was Robert Fitzroy who in 1854 became the first head of the
newly formed Meteorological Office. Fitzroy's rules for deducing what
weather may be in store from the appearance of clouds and the colour
of the sky are familiar to all weather prophets.

We entered the Second Narrows late that evening and at 10 p.m.,
in teeming rain, anchored in the lee of Elizabeth Island. This island,
which the Chileans call Isla Isabel, was named by Drake who had
anchored there in August 1578. In Henry's *Collection of Voyages* we read:

> On August 20th they entered the Straits of Magellan in which they
> struggled with contrary winds, and the various dangers which the
> intricacy of that winding passage exposed them to. When they had
> passed the narrows and had entered a wider sea, they discovered an
> island to which they gave the name of Elizabeth, in honour of their
> sovereign.

Royal Road and Pelican Passage, on the west and south side respec-
tively of Elizabeth Island, were also named by Drake, but his ship, the
Pelican, had by then been given a new name. Apparently, upon reaching the entrance to the Straits, he had renamed her *Golden Hind*, in
remembrance of his friend Christopher Hatton whose crest was a hind.
It is very remarkable, and exemplifies Drake's boldness and skill as a
navigator, that he not only passed through the Straits in winter when

the days are short and the winds strong, but that he took only sixteen days. On this Henry, who published his *Voyages* in 1774, remarks: 'A passage the more extraordinary, as none of our late voyagers made it in less than thirty-six days in the middle of summer.'

By 9 a.m. on a fair morning, with a fair wind, we had Punta Arenas in sight. Some snow-drifts still lay on the hills above. We arrived at noon, a month out from Montevideo. Making for the inshore end of the wooden jetty, just before reaching our chosen berth alongside a small fishing vessel, the only vacant place, we took the ground. It was almost the same spot where on our departure in 1955 we had suffered a like embarrassment. It is natural that such incidents, moments of failure or ignominy, should be more easily and more vividly remembered than our moments of success because the former are so much the more common. On that unlucky occasion a crowd of at least thirty friends and well wishers had assembled to watch us depart, a crowd that by *Mischief*'s standard of publicity amounted to a multitude. We let go our warps, the multitude raised a reedy cheer, we waved our hands airily, when, lo and behold, we were hard and fast aground, where we remained, within a few yards of our embarrassed friends, for the next hour.

On the present occasion a touch of the engine soon got us off and we moved round to the west side of the jetty where several small naval craft lay. A naval tug with the odd name of *Colo Colo* invited us to secure alongside which we did. The Chilean navy were here in force, a cruiser and several frigates lying anchored in the roads. Punta Arenas is a naval base, there is a naval barracks, a small dockyard, and an old four-masted hulk moored in the roads is used as a prison for naval defaulters. In 1955, armed with an introduction from the Chilean naval attache in London, we had received a lot of help from the navy at Punta Arenas. Indeed there was talk of putting a naval officer on board to pilot us through the channels, an idea that, upon seeing *Mischief* they relinquished. We had no introductions this time and they were not needed. *Colo Colo* invited us on board for showers, and the commander of another naval vessel made us a present of two forty-gallon drums of oil. One of these had to be left behind as I did not relish carrying any deck cargo on our next leg. The Chilean navy maintain the Chilean antarctic bases and we learnt from a vessel that had recently returned that the South Shetlands were free of ice.

In Cumberland Sound, South Georgia, approaching King Edward Cove;
Mike Edwards getting lead line ready

Had it not been for the development of the oil field I doubt if I should have noticed much change in Punta Arenas since 1955. Although nowadays there is everywhere a general exodus from the countryside to swell the population of the towns, around Punta Arenas there are no villages and no rural inhabitants to be attracted. Beyond Punta Arenas, as Sir Fopling Flutter said of Hyde Park, 'all is desert'. Owing, no doubt, to the oil field there has been some building of new houses and new shops. The town never had any pretension to beauty so that no development of this kind can make it any worse. By the jetty new warehouses and a post office had sprung up, and one noted landmark, the *Bar Antartica*, a saloon of appropriately forbidding aspect, had been swept away—as also the old *Hotel de France* where our cook of those days, Van Tromp, used to play the piano, and where we had made some memorable meals off the succulent spider crab, or 'centolla', a crab peculiar to these waters. The new houses were all of very modern design and happily no towering blocks of flats have yet been built. Punta Arenas has a strong climate, days when it is not blowing half a gale or more are few, so that high buildings might well be too draughty. Supermarkets have, of course, appeared to make shopping more inhuman and shoppers like things on a conveyor-belt; and there is a new, flash hotel where no one, least of all our friend Van Tromp, would dream of playing the piano.

The British Consulate still transacted decreasing business in the same dingy building that also houses the British Club, even more moribund, and sad to see. Ichabod, the glories are departed! In its hey-day, before the opening of the Panama Canal, Punta Arenas was practically a British colony, the *estancias* of Patagonia and Tierra del Fuego were nearly all British-owned, as was most of the shipping that passed through the Straits and the coal that the ships called for. English was more useful than Spanish, wages were paid in sterling. The late Mr T. P. Jones, British consul at the time of our first visit, who had himself experienced those halcyon days, told me that then no Chilean soldiers or sailors were to be seen in the streets, there was no Customs House, the poorest workmen smoked Abdulla cigarettes, and that whisky and champagne cost five shillings a bottle. For the British community, at any rate, the millenium had already arrived.

The hospitable *Colo Colo* left next day and we moved back to the east side of the jetty alongside a crab-fisher. We bought two centolla for about fifteen shillings. As Herbert, the economist, remarked: 'For that money you become a good, fat chicken.' That day a new figure made his appearance. A Norwegian vessel *Hardanger* came in and one of her deckhands, a young Canadian, Louis, visited *Mischief*. He showed the keenest desire to join us; adventure, he said, and a more intimate knowledge of the sea than can be had from a 10,000-ton steamer, were what he wanted. He had left father to look after the Saskatchewan farm while he went globe-trotting on the cheap. Such a strong, young chap, would, I thought, be a useful acquisition and would be an insurance against Carreo's possible departure. Together we went on board *Hardanger* to learn if his captain would pay him off there and then. The captain refused to do this but agreed that it might be managed at Buenos Aires where they would be in four days. We left it at that. If Louis got his discharge he would cable me and fly down to join us. While on board I had a look at his quarters, a spacious cabin to himself, radiator, fan, washbasin, the lot.

During our stay of ten days we were obliged to shift our berth at least seven times. Whichever side of the jetty we lay, sooner or later the wind would start blowing us hard against it. Whenever the bashing looked like becoming severe we moved out and anchored. Except for the difficulty over the dinghy we should have done better to stay there, but the crew came and went when they pleased and sometimes remained on shore all night. In these circumstances I did not like being long away from the boat. We lost all our fenders and had to replace them with tyres picked up on the beach. Edward Allcard, the singlehander, had apparently suffered as much as we did: a note which he had left for me was appropriately headed: 'Sea Wanderer, Pier Basher, Punta Arenas.'

Allcard had wintered, as he described it, in Beagle Channel, and had sailed from Punta Arenas for Valparaiso three weeks before we arrived. He knew that we were due and had assumed that we would be following him northbound through the Straits and the Channels.

His note to me therefore ran as follows: '... Hope I will have the pleasure of meeting you. I am now leaving for Port Gallant. In January 1767 the master of *Swallow* climbed to the highest summit and deposited a bottle under a cairn, and I might have a look for it. I will paint a white arrow on some prominent rock pointing to a spot below which will be a note for you.' The master of *Swallow* was Carteret who set out from England for a voyage round the world in company with Wallis in the ship *Dolphin*. In Henry's *Voyages* I find this reference:

> ... Came to an anchor in the bay near Cape Gallant, where they catched wild duck in such numbers as to afford them very seasonable relief. Near this spot are very high mountains, one of which was climbed by the master of the *Swalloe*, with the hope of getting a view of the South Sea; but being disappointed in his expectation, he erected a pyramid, and having written the ship's name and the date of the year, he left the same with a shilling within the structure.

Finding arrows painted on rocks and picking up notes in remote places like Port Gallant is right up my street. There is nothing I should have enjoyed more. But unless we went west through the Straits and back round Cape Horn it would be well off our course. However, the story has a sequel. On returning to England I found another letter from Edward Allcard which I again take the liberty of quoting:

> Re the mountain in Port Gallant, between two gales I was lucky enough to reach the summit—the bottle left by Wallis' squadron had been pinched by American tourists 117 years ago, and they had left a copper plaque which I pinched in turn, plus what might have been the remains of Wallis' flagpole. The summit was a most satisfactory one, a sharp serrated ridge which I could sit astride, although the rock whizzing away under my left foot lowered my morale a couple of points. I built you a cairn on the shore, axed a tree to mark it and hoisted a rather nice face towel. Your letter I put in an upturned NIDO milk can telling you I had been lucky.

After receiving that I felt under strong obligations to one day visit Port Gallant. One would love to know whether or not some latter day American tourists have also pinched Allcard's NIDO milk can. I have never heard of tourists in those regions, but unlikelier things have happened. American tourists are now being taken to the Antarctic.

I spent one day away from the ship when a mountaineering friend, Derek Walker, then head of the English school at Punta Arenas, drove three of us out to Fort Bulnes and Port Famine. The country south and west of Punta Arenas is not attractive, lying on the border between the arid flats of Atlantic Patagonia and the uninhabited, densely forested, mountainous regions of Pacific Patagonia, the dividing point being Cape Froward at the southernmost tip of the American continent. On the foothills where forest had grown, the trees have all been felled or burnt and all along the inland side of the unmade road there is mile upon mile of charred stumps. Occasionally one passed a house, or rather a tin shanty, with a grass field enclosed by a broken-down fence. Fort Bulnes is the reconstruction of an old Chilean fort and a popular place with the citizens of Punta Arenas for their Sunday outings. Although it is now merely a historic monument and museum it is still firmly held by the Army who require visitors to first obtain a pass. Port Famine has a longer history but there is nothing there now except the newly built clubhouse of a skin-diving club—almost the last activity that one would expect to see flourishing in Magellan Straits. In 1581, alarmed by Drake's incursion, the Spanish sent an expedition under Sarmiento to fortify the Straits. One would have thought that for this purpose only at the First Narrows would it be any use; nevertheless, a settlement was made at this useless spot, a fort built, and the place named Ciudad del Rey Filipe. Six years later, when Cavendish called there, on the third circumnavigation of the world, nothing remained but 'four cannon and several churches', and the putrefying corpses of the garrison. Four hundred men and thirty women had starved to death. Cavendish called the place Port Famine.

On December 3rd, a Saturday, Louis arrived by air from Buenos Aires as arranged. No sooner had he got his gear on board than a strong westerly blow obliged us to haul off and anchor. On the Sunday we were back alongside and on the Monday, when I had planned to sail, a strong easterly wind discouraged that idea and again drove us off to anchor... We were all ready to go, water and stores on board, and the ship 'entered out', in the curious phrase of shipping agents. Through the good offices of the vice-consul we had a good supply of 'tostada', but no *Nautical Almanac* for 1967 had been obtainable.

CHAPTER VII

TO THE SOUTH SHETLANDS

T HE FURTHER A MAN GOES, the more reluctant he naturally becomes to turn back. As might have been expected, the thought of tamely giving up at this stage was unbearable, even when weighed against the bleak prospect of sailing south with a disgruntled and discordant crew. Only a mutiny on their part could have persuaded me to think differently and they had not yet reached that stage. Though the prime objective had long since been given up, a voyage to the South Shetlands could be regarded as a reconnaissance, either for myself or for some future party, and I had still some hope that Tom and I might do something on Livingston Island, provided we found a secure anchorage. Moreover only some 800 miles now separated us from our goal, albeit the greater part of those miles lay across the cold and reputedly stormy waters of Drake Passage.

This sea between Cape Horn and the South Shetlands is too wide to be called a Strait, as sometimes it is, and its name reminds us that Drake was the first to sail upon it, thus discovering the existence of open water south of the American continent—an entirely fortuitous discovery wrought through the wrath of the winds. It is widely believed that Drake sighted and landed upon Cape Horn, a belief based on the narrative of Fletcher, Drake's chaplain:

> The uttermost cape or headland of all these islands stands near in 56 degrees [Cape Horn is Lat. 55° 59′ S.] without which there is no main or island to be seen southwards, but that the Atlantic Ocean and the South Seas meet in a most large and free scope.

The devious track and the various positions of the *Golden Hind* for the next fifty days after September 8th, when she passed from the Straits of Magellan into the Pacific, are not at all clear, for a sequence of heavy gales drove her hither and yon somewhere to the west and south of the

Horn. In his book *Cape Horn* Felix Reisenberg has plotted the various courses and positions of the Golden Hind during those fifty stormy days from the brief log kept by Drake's Portuguese pilot Nuno da Silva, a better guide probably than the chaplain. His conclusion is that the southernmost island that Drake landed on was 200 miles west and south of Cape Horn in Lat. 57° S. It is unfortunate that no such island now exists, but as Reisenberg points out, the position coincides with Burnham or Pactolus bank where the water shoals from 2000 fathoms to 70 fathoms. He accounts for its disappearance either by volcanic activity or the wear and tear of three hundred years of pounding by heavy seas and, no doubt, icebergs. It is an interesting theory, incapable of either proof or disproof.

The prevailing weather conditions in Drake Passage are thus described in the *Antarctic Pilot*:

> North of about Lat. 60° S. winds from some westerly direction strongly predominate, and their mean force is high. The 'Roaring Forties' is a well-known term to navigators in the southern hemisphere for the strong, predominantly westerly winds which prevail south of Lat. 40° S. The name might seem to imply that the winds were less strong south of Lat. 50° S., but this is not so. In most sectors the westerly winds continue unabated as far south as about Lat. 55° S., and in many sectors, in January, nearly to Lat. 60° S. Any decrease in velocity south of Lat. 55° S. is not so much a real decrease in speed as an increase in variability. Considering average conditions, the circum-polar trough [a line of minimum mean pressure] is the limit of the predominantly westerly winds and south of this [normally Lat. 60° to 65° S.] easterlies predominate. Gales are most frequent in the zone of the Westerlies to the north of the circum-polar trough. Observations from whaling ships show that gales reach a frequency exceeding 20% in places between Lat. 40° S. and 55° S., and that they generally decrease in frequency with increasing latitude to a minimum in Lat. 63° S.

Lat. 63° S., by the way, is about the latitude of the South Shetlands so that we should be heading for a region of comparative calms. Bearing in mind the wind conditions I had thought preferable to make

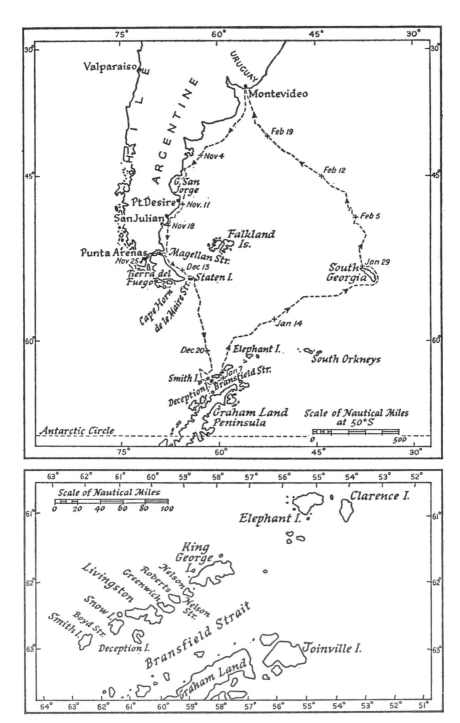

Map 2: Track chart for Southern Ocean expedition:
Montevideo—Southern Ocean; The South Shetland Islands

our departure for the south from Punta Arenas rather than from Port Stanley in the Falkland Islands, on the ground that we should start with some 200 miles of westing in hand. However, if the winds ran true to form, as they so seldom do, the advantage is less apparent, indeed there would be nothing in it. For having first been swept away to the east, when we reached Lat. 60° S., we should conveniently be swept back again by the predominant Easterlies. Happily *Mischief* is not a cork to be swept about at the mercy of winds and waves as such calculations might imply. Except when hove-to we have some control over her direction, and in mid-summer, even in those latitudes, one need not expect to be hove-to for days on end. It might therefore have been as easy and more politic to call at Port Stanley to make our number there, since the islands we were bound for are part of the Falkland Islands Dependencies. We were, I believe, expected there and our failure to turn up may in part have accounted for the coolness of our reception at Deception Island.

We got our anchor at 8 a.m. and sailed away unnoticed. With the ebb tide still under us we carried on to the Second Narrows through which we passed escorted by a large school of Commerson's dolphins,* a species peculiar to these waters, some five to six feet long and genuine piebalds. The grace and speed of these lithe creatures, clearly visible in the smooth, pale green water, held us fascinated and kept our cameras busy; but I strongly suspect that one of them snatched our left-hand rotator which disappeared about this time. For the rest of the voyage outwards and homewards we dispensed with a patent log, making the man on watch responsible for recording his estimate of what mileage the boat had sailed during his watch. The tide turned against us as we left the Narrows and we did not come to an anchor in Gregory Bay until after midnight. While sounding our way up to the anchorage Tom hove the lead

---

* Commerson's dolphin (*Cephalorhymhus commersonii*) is perhaps the most conspicuously marked small cetacean to be found in the Southern Ocean. It has the alternative common names of piebald porpoise and Le Jacobite, the latter Commerson's own name for it; both refer to the striking black and white colour of the body. It has been observed in the Straits of Magellan, near Tierra del Fuego, and at the Falkland Islands.

without making it fast with the result that we lost the lead-line and its 7-lb. lead.

Next morning we passed the First Narrows and anchored again a few miles beyond, where we remained for the rest of the day and the night waiting for a fair wind. Shortly after starting on the following day we sighted the R.R.S. *Shackleton* which altered course to close us, her deck crowded with bearded figures peering at us from behind cameras. Next day she passed us again bound south having made a quick turn-round at Punta Arenas where she had called to land a sick man from one of the Antarctic bases. On neither occasion did they speak to us. One could not but feel that they regarded us with a faint air of disapproval.

The weather behaved in its usual erratic way, the wind hanging obstinately in the east, bringing with it a lot of rain and some fog. By the third day since leaving the Straits we had got only as far as Rio Grande where there is a large 'frigorifico' and a wireless station. The Rio Grande marks the dividing line between the pampas country of the northern part of Tierra del Fuego, where the sheep-runs are, from the mountainous regions to the south. At last we got a breeze from the west, hoisted the twins and ran fast to the south-east. At 8 p.m., wind and sea having increased, we reefed the twins, and when I came on at midnight we were north of the entrance to Straits de la Maire. These straits were first discovered and traversed in 1616 by a small Dutch private expedition that had been launched mainly with the hope of breaking the monopoly of the Dutch East India Company by finding a new route to the Far East. Two ships, *Unity* and *Hoorn*, sailed from the port of Hoorn with Schouten in command and the two brothers Le Maire on board. Their father, Isaac Le Maire, who had quarrelled with the East India Company, had been the moving spirit behind the voyage. While careened at Port Desire having the weed burnt off, the smaller of the two ships, *Hoorn*, caught fire and became a total loss. *Unity* went on through the Straits de la Maire and was the first to round the cape to which Schouten gave the name Hoorn.

Dangerous tide rips extend for many miles from both sides of the entrance to the straits, and when southbound it is necessary to enter at high water. I much wanted to pass through the straits but not only had we ill-timed our arrival; we should have to lower the twins, set the main, and steer south with a biggish sea on the beam. There are never any lack of reasons or excuses for inaction. I decided to leave well alone and to carry on eastwards along the north shore of Staten Island. In the morning we had glimpses of the lower slopes of this mountainous island, thickly clad in Antarctic beech, glimpses that were soon blotted out by cloud. According to some doubtful sights we were ten miles east of the island when the wind dropped. The glass had fallen to twenty-nine inches, so we set the trysail fully expecting a dirty night. Nothing came of this but next morning with the island still in sight, we lay tumbling in a horribly confused sea for many hours making no progress at all. The meeting of the current coming round Cape Horn with that through the various channels of Tierra del Fuego causes an unusually agitated sea off the coasts of Staten Island. As the *Pilot* warns: 'There are very dangerous overfalls off the eastern extremity of the island when the wind is against the tidal steam; they have been reported to extend 18 miles from the island.'

Given a knowledge of Spanish and the right frequency one could no doubt receive weather forecasts from the Rio Grande station. As we were not so equipped we were not liable to be frightened by any forecasts. The warnings of the barometer are at least silent but in a small boat, when the sails can be handed and all made snug in a few minutes, one sometimes wonders whether they too could not be dispensed with. Why disturb one's peace of mind by trying to peer into the immediate future? 'Let us cease to consider what may never happen,' said Dr Johnson, 'and what when it shall happen will laugh at human speculation.' It seemed to be the custom in these parts for the wind to fall light as the barometer fell, and only when the barometer rose did things begin to happen. On the 15th it fell to 28.6 inches, and that evening, when it had started to rise, the wind came in so hard that we set the trysail and double-reefed the staysail. Whereupon the wind began to moderate. It had become noticeably colder, the air temperature 36° F. and the sea 39° F., and we shifted into our winter woollens. We had minor worries besides the cold. First the cabin heater, which burns diesel oil, caught fire and had to be extinguished with the help of one of our appliances, and then the lavatory got blocked. I was glad to see that our marine engineer Carreo made no bones about tackling this.

I'm afraid that by now Carreo thoroughly disliked us all, with a special aversion for Mike Edwards whose blond hair and beard he

The whaling station, Grytviken, South Georgia;
old hulk and whalebones in foreground

Old try-pots outside the manager's house, Grytviken, South Georgia

may have found provocative. He seldom opened his mouth except to quarrel. In arranging the watches I took care to precede him so that I was the one to call him. When woken in the middle of the night he might be in a belligerent mood and he would be less likely to start a fight with me than with one of the others. Herbert had developed such a crop of boils that he could not work on deck and had to revert to the galley, but in spite of all remained remarkably cheerful. Since neither of these two had much in the way of warm clothing we all subscribed what we could spare towards their wardrobe. Tom, who so far had been most loyal, now turned sour. He claimed that had he known we were to attempt no landing on Smith Island he would not have left Punta Arenas. Ignorant of what the people at the British base on Deception Island were like, I promised that if we found a climber among them, as seemed likely, he could accompany Tom while I looked after the boat. I felt sure that a man would be allowed time off for such an enterprise.

Books about sailing ships in the waters south of Cape Horn naturally lay stress on the gales encountered, so that one is left with the impression that gales seldom cease and that seas are always mountainous. At first one thinks that 5000 miles of ocean unbroken by any land must inevitably give birth to gigantic waves, forgetting that the depressions, and the winds that cause the waves, probably extend over less than 500 miles. One imagines, too, that in the seemingly infrequent lulls between gales an endless procession of great combers, the Cape Horn greybeards, marches on relentlessly from the west. This is not so. The sea behaves here as elsewhere, and when the wind is not blowing, as happens frequently in summer, there are no waves. From my own very limited experience of four voyages in the Southern Ocean I should say that in summer the gales of the Roaring Forties, Furious Fifties, and Shrieking Sixties, are no more frequent or fierce than in similar latitudes in the North Atlantic. Gale frequencies may well be higher off the pitch of the Horn, as is generally the way off capes at the extremities of great land masses, like the Cape of Good Hope (the so-called Cape of Storms), Cape Leeuwin, and the Snares. But in the southern hemisphere these latitudes are colder than their northern equivalents and more cloudy.

With a beam wind and a smooth sea we had a fine run of 100 miles on December 18th, a pleasant enough day except for a snow shower which lasted about half an hour. That night we crossed what is known as the Antarctic convergence, marked by a sudden fall in sea temperature, the boundary between the colder, less saline Antarctic water to the south, and the warmer more saline sub-antarctic water. Overnight the sea temperature dropped from 39° to 35° F., and next day to 33° F., where it remained until we had recrossed the convergence on the way homewards. In a paper to the Royal Geographical Society, Dr Dilwyn John, of the *Discovery II* expedition, thus vividly described the meaning of the Antarctic convergence:

One might well ask, what can this boundary be, far away in the open sea? It might be supposed that sea-water throughout the oceans mixed readily, that there would be something like an even and gradual transition from the water of minus temperature, poor in salts because of melting ice and falling snow, at the Antarctic ice-edge, to the warm water rich in salts in the tropic. It is not so: there are successive zones from north to south separated by sharp boundaries. Antarctic surface water is very cold, and although it is poor in salts it is heavier than the warmer more saline water of the neighbouring zone to the north, the temperate zone of the southern hemisphere. This temperate zone is called the sub-antarctic. Now Antarctic water moves for the most part towards the east because of the prevailing westerly winds, but it has a northern movement too. Where it meets sub-antarctic water the very different densities of the two do not allow of ready mixing, and the heavier Antarctic water sinks sharply below the lighter sub-antarctic and continues its flow northwards below it.

This line along which the heavy Antarctic surface water meets the lighter surface water and sinks below it, is the boundary in the surface of the open sea that I spoke of. It is called the Antarctic convergence. It is a physical boundary very easily and precisely detected with a thermometer by the sharp change in temperature as one passes from one zone to another. It can be detected as easily if not so precisely by a zoologist with a tow-net because each of the two waters has a distinctive fauna of floating animal life. But we, whether

sailors or zoologists, know and will remember the convergence best
in another way; as the line to the north of which we felt one day, after
months in the Antarctic, genial air again and soft rain like English
rain in the spring. In the southernmost lands in the sub-antarctic,
the islands about Cape Horn, the earth smells as earth should smell
and as it never does in the Antarctic. It is no doubt the north-easterly
course of the convergence between the longitudes of Cape Horn
and South Georgia, so that the former is left far to the north and the
latter to the south, that accounts for the vast difference in the climate
of two islands that are precisely in the same latitude and only 1000
miles apart. The lower slopes of Staten Island are clothed with beech
trees with so rich an undergrowth that it is difficult to push through.
South Georgia, the other island, is a true Antarctic land. The snow
line of South Georgia is lower than the tree line of Tierra del Fuego.

On December 19th we had a good run of ninety miles under the twin
staysails, an unusual rig for these waters, and by next day I reckoned we
were about ninety miles north of Livingston Island. The wind increased
that night so that at 2 a.m., when two small icebergs were sighted, we
hove-to on account of the wind and the poor visibility. In this latitude,
62° S., it never became properly dark, only the two hours either side of
midnight were a bit murky. Deception Island lies to the south-west of
Livingston Island and the approach to it from the north is guarded by
a chain of islands stretching for nearly two hundred miles from Smith
Island in the west to King George Island in the east. The northern side
of the chain abounds with islets, rocks, and breakers, and most of the
islands are separated by comparatively narrow channels, so that the
only safe and sensible approach for strangers like ourselves is by the
twenty-mile wide Boyd Strait between Smith Island and Snow Island.
It had become increasingly rare for us to get a reliable sight, especially
noon sights for the all-important latitude. Either it would be cloudy,
raining, snowing, or foggy, and on one occasion, having already had
the sextant dowsed with spray, I found that the wind made my eyes
water too much to take a sight. Not that one need complain about difficulties that must be expected and allowed for when by choice one
visits such regions. As Byron said: 'Comfort must not be expected by
folk who go a-pleasuring.'

Having been hove-to for most of the 21st, when by dead reckoning we were twenty-five miles north of Livingston Island, we let draw in the evening in fog, visibility less than half a mile. But by next morning we were again hove-to in a heavy sea and south-easterly gale, the weather too thick for us to see anything except two moderately large icebergs. By now we were more than a little uncertain of our position. Snow Island should have been only a few miles away and with the wind at south-east we were drifting safely away from it. In order to lessen the drift we tried out a parachute anchor I had brought for just such a contingency. On the voyage to Heard Island, such an anchor, a twenty-nine-foot diameter parachute on five fathoms of anchor chain, had held *Patanela*, a boat twice as heavy as *Mischief*, more or less stationary for an hour in a severe gale. Finally the fitting between the cable and the parachute had parted, but the parachute itself remained intact. The material of our present parachute must have been inferior or maybe it got foul of the cable. In five minutes we were hauling inboard its tattered remnants. Normally when hove-to one might expect to drift twenty-five to thirty miles in twenty-four hours, a distance well worth trying to save.

That it never became completely dark did something to lessen the anxiety that a stormy night naturally inspires. I had a chill and stood no watch and might have enjoyed the luxury of undisturbed sleep had it not been for the whining and howling of the wind. Only by plugging one's ears could the mournful and nerve-racking dirge played by the wind upon the rigging be shut out, and then one would be fearful of missing some more significant noise—a hail from the deck, the breaking of a skylight, or some worse disaster. Long before there is any reasonable hope of the gale abating one begins to time the intervals between the gusts, in the hope that if the lulls lengthen the wind is taking off. The glass remained high and steady throughout and each lull served only to make the next gust sound fiercer. The wind by itself is of less consequence than the sea it raises, except that its noise, like the noise of a bombardment, in time wears a man down. In the open sea waves have to build up to twenty feet or more before their breaking crests become dangerous to a small boat, however seaworthy, and if the wind blows hard enough for long enough this is bound to happen. Whether hove-to or running, the chance of being hit by a breaking sea is always there, and though a bad helmsman can increase the chances, a good one cannot do much to lessen them. Not all seas run true, on a dark night a man cannot see, and a heavy boat like *Mischief* is not quick enough on the helm for a man to take avoiding action.

On the afternoon of the following day, when still hove-to, we had to lower the mainsail to repair a seam. When it is reefed right down the sail and the massive boom are not too difficult to control even in a hard blow. Even though the wind had blown steadily for twenty-four hours the sea had in it no real malice. The wind, even in gusts, had not risen above force 9 and since it was blowing from south-east the sea had no long fetch. Our steady drift away from the islands caused us some concern but it would have been far greater had we been drifting towards them. On the early morning of December 24th we let draw again and sailed slowly southwards in cold, wet fog. When the wind died we continued southwards under the engine until a fresh fall in the barometer frightened me into stopping to await clearer weather. For three days we had had no reliable sights and our rate of drift could only be guessed at. We might be in Boyd Strait, for all I knew, between Smith and Snow Islands, not a good place to be in if another gale started either from east or west. In fact, as the next day showed, we had enough sea-room.

On Christmas morning at 3 a.m. the fog rolled away, revealing to my surprised gaze an unbroken horizon, no land anywhere in sight. I put the visibility at about ten miles so that had we been near Smith or Snow Islands, as I thought, we should certainly have seen something. This clearing did not last long. A wind sprang up from north-east, bringing in its train sleet and rain, and with this fine quartering breeze we sailed southwards at four knots. If we missed the islands, we could hardly miss the Antarctic continent some sixty miles beyond. Long before breakfast I had to call all hands to change the main for the trysail, a call that they did not respond to with much alacrity; not for the first time I sensed how bloody-minded they were becoming. And, Christmas Day though it was, I felt out of humour, angry with myself more than with anyone for not knowing where we were. In the brief diary I kept, I notice that under the heading 'Christmas Day' there is the query, 'My worst?' It had a faint resemblance to Christmas Day 1955 when we were not exactly lost but in doubt about our next move. We were in a tent on the Calvo glacier, dining largely off pemmican, uncertain as to whether we should find any route ahead or be forced to retreat to the boat. It is not so much where you are that matters but whom you are with, and on that occasion I had two staunch companions.

Meantime snow began to fall and the cabin heater created another diversion for us. After Carreo had tried in vain to make it burn, Herbert had a go and was only too successful, setting the whole thing on fire. The extinguishers finally subdued it, but their fumes made the cabin untenable for some time. Thus we were all on deck, but it was Tom, I think, who first sighted land. Vaguely through the murk, not much more than a mile away, we saw a white blur with a dense black rock to one side of it. This most welcome and dramatic landfall we took at first to be Snow Island, which has off its western shore the 500-foot-high Castle Rock. But as we drew nearer our 'Castle Rock' became a part of the island, a part too steep to hold snow, and we realized that the broken glacier we looked at, and the steep snow slopes above, must be descending from high, cloud-hidden peaks. It could only be Smith Island, a magnificent landfall achieved entirely by accident. We closed the shore, if an ice-cliff lapped by the sea can be called a shore, and had to stand out again when the wind showed signs of failing. Before the weather closed in, as it did when the wind died, we had time to discern what looked like a cape to the north-east. We confidently hoped that this was Cape Smith at the northern extremity of the island, for the island is twenty miles long from north to south and we were on the wrong side, that is the west side of it. From some hidden store Herbert produced a bottle of beer and we had buns for tea, thus thriftily celebrating both Christmas Day and a successful landfall. Having started the engine we soon rounded what proved to be Cape Smith and set a course for Deception Island some sixty miles to the east. After supper, the fog having become dense, we stopped.

'There is something personal and compact about an island, no matter how desolate it may be.' These words of Shackleton, which probably applied to Elephant Island where his party took refuge, seemed to me equally applicable to Smith Island. It is as compact as could be, no bays, inlets, or fjords, as desolate an island as any I have seen, and it had a grim enough personality even though some 5000 feet of its more daunting aspect remained hidden. In the very short distance that we coasted along it, sheer ice cliffs, glacier tongues, rock cliffs, or boulders, forbade even the thought of a landing. Yet somewhere along that considerable coastline there must be some kind of a cove and a beach. To search for it from a small boat might take days and would involve the risk of being caught in a gale on the wrong side of the island; for it would not be easy, in view of its twenty-mile length, to nip quickly round to the lee side. And having found a landing place there is the problem of the 6900-foot Mount Foster which unfortunately we never saw. It would be too much to expect that the landing place would also be the most convenient spot from which to tackle the mountain. In mountaineering the means are more important than the end, so that one must hope that this rich prize does not fall to some party that has been landed conveniently adjacent to the mountain by helicopter.

It is a great pity that no logbook or account of James Weddell's 1820 voyage has been found or is now likely to be found. Where he made his landing on Smith Island is not known. His later voyage, when he penetrated deep into the Weddell Sea, is described in his own book *A Voyage towards the South Pole* published in 1825, and in this book occurs the brief reference to his having landed on Smith Island: 'Of the South Shetlands, the highest and most forbidding in aspect is the western island which in 1820 I named James Island as I was the first who landed upon it.' Dr Brian Roberts, of the Scott Polar Institute, assures me that James and Smith Island are the same. It had been discovered by William Smith in 1819 and it was his name that the British sealers used during the next few years until it became firmly established. These early sealers either did not know of Weddell's name (which was not published until 1825) or they knowingly used the earlier name.

CHAPTER VIII

AT DECEPTION ISLAND

NEXT MORNING, in the absence of any wind, we began motoring, intent upon reaching Deception Island that day. Although the fog had thinned we were too far away to see anything of either Smith, Snow Island, or Deception. We had not been motoring for long when a wind from the north-east set in but by then the island had become dimly discernible and we made haste to close it. When we had got up to South Point the wind had developed into a snow blizzard and we were faced with a three-mile plug into the teeth of it north along the coast. The entrance to Port Foster is narrow and in our anxiety not to miss it we kept within a quarter mile of the low steep cliffs which even at that range were frequently blotted out by snow squalls. At times we seemed to stand still. Driving into the blizzard from dead ahead, and a short, steep sea, the engine just managed to push us along at about one knot. Thus it was late afternoon before we were off the entrance to Neptune's Bellows and in the most welcome lee of the high cliffs to the east of it. The crew emerged from the unheated cabin to see the sights while I at last felt some life returning to my half-frozen hands, having been steering since we sighted the island.

Neptune's Bellows is the name given to the entrance to Port Foster by American sealers in the early years of the nineteenth century. The name is suggestive enough for sailors, but in point of fact, both on the day we entered and the day we left, the Bellows were not working. Even with a north-easterly blizzard blowing outside we met no furious blasts inside the Bellows, and on the day we sailed out the wind barely filled the sails. Nevertheless, the striking scenery at the entrance fully merits so imaginative a name, for on both sides are high cliffs of vividly coloured red and yellow rock. That on the north side is a true, uncompromising cliff, the rock rising vertically out of the sea for two or three hundred feet; the south side is less sheer and on a smaller scale. The width between these cliffs is about three cables but the navigable width is only half this, for in mid-channel there is a sunken rock. On the south shore lies the forlorn, rusty wreck of a whale chaser, a strong hint to the stranger to stick close to the north side of the channel.

Deception Island, like most of the neighbouring islands, is of volcanic origin, and is one of the few volcanoes that have been breached and inundated by the sea. It is for all the world like an atoll, Port Foster representing the lagoon and Neptune's Bellows the pass; but the surrounding reef, instead of coral, is a ridge of a mean height of 1000 feet permanently covered with snow, the rim of the original volcano. Despite Byron's, 'Damn description, it is always disgusting', the following details from the *Antarctic Pilot* will be of interest:

> The whole island is of volcanic origin, forming one of the largest and most remarkable crater islands in the world. The principal rock is lava. Brickstone is dispersed upon the beaches and in large fragments on the hills, giving relief to the dull scenery. Numerous hot sulphurous springs occur, the temperature of the hottest from 185° to 190° F., hot enough to boil an egg. In January 1936 the hottest water found in Whalers Bay was 127° F. in a brackish stream flowing down the beach near the whaling station. At low tide the temperature of the sea along the shore was 95° F. At high tide the temperature of the sea at this point was 43.5° F., but one cable offshore it was 38.5° F. It is reported by the whalers that at times the water in this anchorage has been hot enough to blister the paint on the factory ships. In April 1927, the R.R.S. *Discovery* found much evidence of volcanic activity. Clouds of steam frequently arose at the water line in Whalers Bay and at low-water mark. At 8 inches below the scoriae and ashes on the beach the temperature was found to be 133° F.

Turning sharp right—to starboard, I should say—on emerging from Neptune's Bellows one enters Whalers Bay at the head of which is the British base and the derelict whaling station. We brought up first in unexpectedly shoal water of only 2 fathoms. As this would not do we anchored again in 7 fathoms and immediately began to drag. Unlike the cliffs of Neptune's Bellows, the snow-covered ridge behind the base did not afford much of a barrier to the north-east wind which still blew with great force. The third time we let go, the anchor appeared to be holding so I went below to gather myself together before visiting the base. Meantime Tom and Louis already had the dinghy in the water and were in such haste to get ashore that they were about to push off. Unwilling to be preceded by two such uncouth heralds I hastened to join them. The voyagers who landed on islands inhabited by savages were at first often kindly treated; only later, reasoning perhaps from the uncivil behaviour of their visitors, did the natives turn hostile. So it was with the savages of Deception Island. A reception committee some half-dozen strong gave us a warm welcome, though the base leader himself was not there. As we walked towards the huts a short distance away I remembered to ask if among the dozen or so men at the base there were any climbers, and learnt that there were not. Had there been one he would not have been able to accompany us; no one was even allowed to visit *Mischief.*

We were on the point of entering the hut when, happening to look back, I saw *Mischief* moving rapidly away from the shore with no one on deck. Muttering some hasty apologies to our would-be hosts I turned and ran for the dinghy, to be followed presently by Tom whose seaman's instinct for the moment overcame his ill-will. Louis remained there. We were told later that he had had a bath and used up all their hot water, a fact which conceivably may have contributed to the blighting of our prospects. As Tom and I rowed off in haste to overtake *Mischief* before she fetched up on the opposite shore, our former acquaintance *Shackleton* turned the corner out of Neptune's Bellows. As soon as she had anchored and put a warp ashore her launch came over with an invitation from her captain to lie alongside her for the night, an offer we gladly accepted. They were a cheerful crowd, both the crew and the men bound for the various Antarctic bases, and treated us well. After a hot shower I had a drink with Captain Turnbull who told me that for the last four seasons he had been looking in vain for a possible landing place on Smith Island. He also told me that about three days before Christmas they had visited Port Foster and found it full of pack-ice. At that moment there was not a fragment of ice anywhere.

Port Foster is the Port of Entry for the South Shetlands and the base leader is also the resident magistrate. Accordingly I went ashore next day with the ship's papers and crew's passports. Christmas, or Boxing Day, had apparently exhausted the stock of goodwill at the base. I got no further than the outer office where I had a formal inter-view with the base leader who expressed surprise at our visit and some disgust for Louis and Herbert, for he, too, had been there the previous night for a bath. I mentioned that I would like to buy a small quantity of stores and learnt that it was unlikely that any could be spared. I was surprised at this and had no complaint to make but one could not help comparing the treatment strangers received at similarly remote for-eign bases, where one had not even to ask for anything. At Kerguelen, for example, the French had loaded us with bread, butter, potatoes, enough chocolate to last the voyage home, jars of paté, tins of fruit, all the petrol and paraffin we needed, and finally a barrel of red wine. At Pond Inlet the Royal Canadian Mounted Police post had so stocked us up that we left with more food on board than when the voyage began. At Tingmiarmiut in East Greenland, where seven Danes maintained a weather station, we were shown into their store and told to help ourselves. Such places are usually overstocked, for they keep a year's supply in hand in case of accidents to the relief ship. This may or may not have been the case at Deception Island, but we heard of, and later saw for ourselves, cases of tinned butter, dried eggs, dried milk, dried potatoes, etc. rotting away in one of the several disused oil tanks, once part of the whaling station. These tanks had been holed by the navy in the last war to prevent their possible use by German raiders.

Meantime we enjoyed brief popularity on board *Shackleton* where we had been invited to take our meals in the mess with the British Ant-arctic Survey party. We particularly welcomed this invitation because Carreo had dismantled the stove, strewing the cabin with bits of iron and soot. With the help of one of *Shackleton*'s, engineers he was busy constructing it on a new principle. Though the effects of any action are plain enough, their causes are sometimes obscure; and there were two reasons currently offered for the sudden eclipse of our popularity—no more meals were to be served to *Mischief*'s crew, and a little later Cap-tain Turnbull asked me to move *Mischief* elsewhere. One version was that the wardroom had been left without enough sausages for break-fast, the other that Tom had somehow fallen foul of the captain. Since our arrival I had seen little of Tom who had transferred himself to the seamen's mess where he had been the life and soul of the party. But he had been seen having a short talk with the captain and judging from

Tom's own version of what had passed I was not altogether surprised at being asked to shove off. Before we parted company we filled our water tanks from *Shackleton*'s hose, thus saving a lot of trouble later. She was taking on water from a well on shore. There are several wells and it is said that each whaling ship had its own well. The *Pilot* recommends taking water when the tides are low as occasionally salt water may seep into the well when the tides are high. Captain Turnbull also gave me a chart of South Georgia but could spare none of their 1967 *Nautical Almanacs*. He also assured me, and his position enabled him to give the assurance, that we should be able to buy what stores we needed.

So we anchored once more off the base, this time using our 1-cwt. Fisherman type anchor instead of the 60-lb. CQR anchor which was no use in this bottom of ash and cinders. We also took a line ashore, made fast to a boiler, the debris of the whaling station. Having attended to this I once more sought out the base leader to give him a list of our modest requirements. He was busy with the construction of a small jetty but took time off to give me a lecture on the irresponsibility of sailing a small boat to the Antarctic. He looked like the earnest young head of Dr Whacko's Academy and I felt like a newly joined urchin, too dumbfounded to utter. I can only think that this far-flung Government official, monarch of all he surveyed—provided he ignored the two foreign bases—greatly resented private intruders upon his small domain.

Back on board Mike cleaned up the refuse habitually deposited in the galley by Herbert, and with the stove put together and burning the cabin had become almost inhabitable. Carreo's reconstruction was not a success. It burned dangerously fiercely and gave out volumes of filthy smoke. Rather than perish by fire at sea, or become as black as Eskimos cooking over a blubber fire, we preferred to be cold. Long before reaching South Georgia we gave up using it, and later on had the satisfaction one always finds in throwing things overboard. Louis had now developed boils and since the British base had no doctor, the three of them, Louis, Herbert, and Carreo, walked to the Chilean base three miles away. A dry glacier of black ice, black with cinders, had to be crossed, so mountaineer Tom, who had long dissociated himself from any work on board, showed them the way. They did not go there entirely for their health. As I was told by Louis, whom I had come to regard as a seagoing bum with neither manners nor principles, all three hoped to arrange a passage to Punta Arenas. This hope was not fulfilled, though while we were there a naval tug arrived and departed. Louis attributed his boils to a low diet, the same diet that Mike, Tom, and I had been living on for six months, free from either boils, scurvy, or any other disease. Louis was another example of an adventure-lover who wanted his adventure on a plate without the attendant discomforts or risks. Not only should we have had the latest drugs on board but also a radio transmitter, distress signals, etc.

Shackleton left next day bound south and if any of us had expected her to leave us a sack of potatoes or a few loaves of bread they were disappointed. Some of the B.A.S. party, however, who were particularly friendly, had given us some luxuries from their private stores. Having seen her off Mike, Tom, and I walked over the ridge behind the base to visit a penguin rookery on the east coast. The route lay mostly over hard snow, lying presumably on top of ice, for the snow line is only a little above the beach. There were a few crevasses but they were open and not deep. The Antarctic terns that were nesting along the beach became very aggressive if their nests were approached and repeatedly, as it were, dive-bombed us. There is no grass anywhere on the island, only mosses and lichens that in places form a carpet over what might be mistaken for soil—very light soil, perhaps, as Lord Salisbury once described the Sahara Desert. The rookery was on rocky, snow-free ground a hundred feet above the sea, very noisy and smelly. They were Macaroni penguins, about two feet in height, rather truculent, and smelling like goats. They did not seem to bother with nests but just layed their eggs in any slight depression. None of the eggs were hatched.

We had no further contact with anyone at the base. One or two of them had rowed past in their boat, eyeing us curiously from a safe distance but never coming alongside, much less on board. They must have had their orders. I was therefore surprised when Dr Whacko himself brought off the promised stores—20 lb each of flour and sugar, 5 lb of tea and coffee, thirty gallons of diesel oil, five gallons of paraffin, and one gallon of methylated spirit. It is to his credit that he did not demand cash down, but in due course the bill came and was paid. This visit must have been prompted by curiosity or, perhaps, as may happen to anyone, he had been suddenly overcome with friendly feelings. It was a beastly morning with a cold north-east wind and snow, so when the boat had been unloaded we naturally asked him and his underling on board for a drink. The alacrity with which he accepted surprised us and gave us the warm, satisfying glow felt by those who turn the other cheek, a warmer glow than can be got by retaliating in kind, tempting though that is. Despite two snorts of whisky the conversation remained stilted, consisting mainly of questions on our part about their life at the base. One felt sorry for them, for it must be a damnably dull life on Deception Island with no prospect of travel as there is at some of the bases. One of their jobs, too, was the breeding of huskies to be used for sledge journeys at those bases. They climbed into their boat and we saw no more of Whacko and his academy.

Since Herbert and Louis were daily walking to the Chilean base to have their boils treated I decided to go there and remain until they were reported fit. On the last day of 1966, a fine day with a good sailing breeze, we sailed round, a better way of going there than by walking over a dry glacier. The Chilean base is on the same side of Port Foster at Pendulum Cove, the place where in 1829 Captain Foster, of H.M.S. *Chanticleer*, established his pendulum station and carried out experiments for determining the force of gravity. The cove has since silted up. Where there was once a considerable inlet there is now only a small cove and beyond the beach a freshwater lake. We anchored in six fathoms and put a warp ashore, the wind by now blowing offshore in very violent gusts. Tom and Mike, who heartily despised each other, had a fierce slanging match over the proper way to run out a warp.

The Chilean base is large, modern, and fitted with all conveniences, electric light, hot water, central heating. In summer there are over 100 men there and at the moment they were engaged in building a runway for a seaplane. The Commandant, an Air Force officer, who had already seen something of our quality in the shape of Louis, Carreo, and Herbert, did not welcome me effusively. Still he proved more hospitable than stern, path-of-duty Whacko, inviting us to have our meals in the men's messroom, and to ask for anything we needed.

We had not yet eaten a large, home-made Christmas pudding and new Year's Eve seemed the time to eat it. For twenty minutes I occupied myself in the galley making a rum sauce to help it down, and on returning to the cabin learnt that Mike and Louis had gone ashore to have a fight. This was better, of course, than staging it in the cabin, and their showing so much consideration left me astonished. Nevertheless it boded no good. This crew of mine should have shipped with Fanning, the sealing captain already mentioned. 'It was always with me,' he writes, 'a cardinal duty to state, on shipping of crew, that it must be well understood by them, as a prominent part of our agreement, that all the quarrelling and swearing was to be done by myself and the work by them.' Since they could not devour each other like Kilkenny cats, I rather hoped that Mike would win, but it was not to be. Louis was a bit of a pugilist as well as a bum, he read books on prize-fighting, and presently returned to announce, rather disappointedly, that a couple of punches had been enough for Mike who had refused to return on board with him. I found Mike, now with a fruity black eye, pacing the shore in bewildered fashion, and persuaded him to come back to the boat. Even before this it was clear that the crew hated each other, that we all hated Carreo, and that they were united only by their hatred for me. Except that Dr Johnson himself was by no means hated, our situation reminded me of life in what he had called his seraglio, three elderly, indigent females whom he charitably lodged in his house along with one Levett, an equally indigent, unqualified medical practitioner: 'Mrs Williams hates everybody; Levett hates Mrs Desmoulins and does not love Mrs Williams; Mrs Desmoulins hates them both; Poll loves none of them.'

New Year's Eve continued its eventful way. The crew, less Mike and I, were to go ashore for a party with the Chileans. While they were changing into their best rig, Carreo, already half drunk, made determined efforts to push off by himself in the dinghy. The only way to checkmate him was to take the oars below. Having got rid of them Mike and I had to divide the night for anchor watches, the wind now blowing offshore with gale force. Towards midnight Tom brought off Herbert with news that could not wait, news confided to him secretly by a Chilean friend, that proved to be stupid enough to have been invented by Herbert—so puzzled was the Chilean doctor by Herbert's various ailments, that if we did not sail next day we would probably be put in quarantine for a month.

Leaving me to think this out they re-embarked, missed the warp by which they could have hauled themselves ashore, and were rapidly blown out of the cove, Tom rowing furiously but in vain. We lost sight of them about a cable's length away trying to round a point where they might find a lee. If they failed they would be blown two miles across the bay to somewhere near the Argentine base, that is if the dinghy did not fill and sink in the rough sea further out. I remembered they had no baler. In the morning, the wind still blowing hard, we could see no life on shore where the effects of the New Year's party had evidently been severe. Mike and I discussed the chance of the dinghy surviving a two-mile voyage across the wind-swept bay. I felt ashamed that we had made no effort to go after them, hard though it might have been with only the two of us on board and a wind that might have been too much for our engine to fight against. The suspense lasted until midday when, happening to go on deck, I caught sight of a figure wearing Herbert's unmistakable red balaclava. Later we saw him and Tom walking out beyond the point, where they had evidently got ashore, in order to retrieve the dinghy. In the afternoon all hands came off bringing some eggs and tomatoes as a peace-offering. No more was said or heard of the quarantine problem, had it ever existed outside Herbert's fertile imagination. 'No problema', by the way, was still his favourite, overworked idiom, expressing his unbounded and singularly ill-founded optimism.

The following day being fine with only a light breeze, the crew ashore and no hostilities, I took the opportunity to reeve a new peak halyard, making spare sheets out of the old one. I had lunch in the men's mess—mutton, lentils, pineapple, red wine, and coffee. Carreo, I noted, was evidently regarded as a figure of fun by the Chileans who, of course, had not got to live with him. Three Air Force officers accompanied me on board for a drink. They so much preferred English cigarettes to their own that I gave them a carton of a hundred, part of the 5000 that had been got for David Shaw, our only cigarette smoker. These were fast melting away, either Carreo or Herbert being busy flogging them to the Chileans. In the evening a naval tug arrived and anchored hard by. When their whaler was rowed ashore with a warp, the ship's dog, an Alsatian, jumped overboard and swam ashore with it. The wind having gone round to south-west we were now stern on to the beach, about five yards off and our rudder touching the bottom, so we ran out a kedge anchor to hold her off. At this cove steam rose from along the water's edge and immediately below the surface the sand felt quite hot. Up to 1936 there were hot springs along the beach and large patches of steaming hot sand.

January 3rd was clear, calm, and sunny. Such days, I imagine, are far more common on the Antarctic mainland than on the off-lying islands. So fair a day could not be wasted so for the first and last time I put on some boots and climbed the easy snow slope leading to the ridge, the rim of the old volcano. Behind Pendulum Cove this attains to a height of 1800 feet and is the highest point of the island. Below lay Bransfield Strait, blue enough to have been taken for the Straits of Gibraltar were it not for the numerous icebergs sparkling in the sun. Across the water sixty miles away, though in appearance no more than twenty, were the mountains of Graham Land. Smith Island was in cloud but to the north and close at hand was Livingston Island, dazzling white snow and ice from end to end and from sea to summit. At its eastern end I could see Mount Bowles (3314 feet), the peak I had had in mind as a poor consolation when Smith Island had to be written off. There is said to be a secure anchorage at Livingston Island, though not very close to Mount Bowles, but by this time I had no heart left for climbing and indeed felt reluctant to leave the ship even for a day.

The others, except Carreo, had gone off for the day to visit another penguin rookery at the north-east corner of the island. When they had not returned by nightfall I felt uneasy about them and annoyed, too, because Carreo and I had again to share an anchor watch, the wind having come in strong from south-west. It seemed more likely that they had spent the night at the Argentine base than that any mis-chance had befallen, so in the morning I went ashore to find out, the two bases being in contact by radio. Sure enough they had been there and at midday they turned up, very pleased with themselves, and went straight on shore for lunch. A small snow-covered island is not the place for men to jump ship, otherwise I doubt if *Mischief* would ever have left. But when I named the next day, January 6th, as the day of our departure for South Georgia en route to Cape Town, no objections were raised. Herbert, accompanied by Tom, immediately set out for the Argentine base where he said he must have a blood test. In reply to my objections, he said that for him this was a matter of life or death.

Carreo, who had spent the last twenty-four hours in his bunk, neither eating nor drinking, then took his gear ashore. He was last seen
trudging slowly along the shore evidently bound for the Argentine
base, and late that evening, on their way back, Tom and Herbert found
him floundering in bewildered fashion in a snow drift and brought
him back. On sailing day it took the Chileans a long time to convince
him that he could not stay with them. Late in the evening they escorted
him down to the beach with his kit and a large box of tinned food, his
private sea stores. He had also acquired a crimson, peaked, American-
style cap with a flap that came down over the back of his neck. In spite
of this fine cap, which henceforth never left his head, he looked even
more out of place in these arctic surroundings. Peary took his faithful
negro, the stalwart Matthew Henson, to the North Pole, but our sub-
tropical species did not flourish in high latitudes.

At 7 p.m., to my untold relief, we sailed. In Neptune's Bellows
the wind failed and we drifted slowly past the great cliff now glowing golden red in the light of the setting sun. From the top two men
from the British base watched us go. They did not wave. Perhaps Dr
Whacko had told them not to.

In December 1967, as I wrote this chapter, Deception Island began
to erupt violently. First reports spoke of a threat to the safety of the
British base. My reaction was like that of Churchill's who, on hearing
of the illness of a political opponent, remarked cheerfully, 'Nothing
trivial, I hope'. The threat proved far from trivial. Both the British and,
more regrettably, the Chilean base, had to be abandoned.

CHAPTER IX

SOUTH GEORGIA

M<small>Y ORIGINAL INTENTION</small> had been to sail direct from the South Shetlands to Cape Town, distant about 4000 miles, but with both wind and current in our favour all the way. But by calling at South Georgia we had the slight possibility of finding there a ship and no chance, however slight, of relieving ourselves of Carreo, our black incubus, should be missed.

In a flat calm we started the engine and coasted the south side of Livingston Island, its higher peaks lit by the sun until nearly midnight. Throughout the night we had an escort of penguins, dashing through the water and surfacing like a school of porpoises. Slow moving and awkward enough on land, in the water they are very much at home, as lively and fast as any fish. In the morning, after passing Greenwich and Roberts Islands, both encased completely in ice, we turned north into Nelson Strait between Roberts Island and Nelson Island further east. After Boyd Strait this is one of the easiest passages between the various islands because all the dangers are above water, but it is no place to be in thick weather on account of strong tides and fierce tide rips, not to speak of icebergs. We had some thirty of them in sight. Meeting a strong adverse tide we did not clear the strait until afternoon. Nelson Island, too, is ice-covered except for a few small rock exposures. On Harmony Point, at its north-west corner, there is a refuge hut and a light, and as we passed it two helicopters flew low over us and landed there. Just as sail had to give way to steam, so the dog team and sledge of the heroic days of Antarctic travel are yielding to aircraft. Had helicopters been in use in Kipling's day his lament for the passing of Romance might have read:

> Farewell! Romance, the skipper said:
> He vanished with the oil we burn,
> And the helicopters overhead.

For a week the weather remained fair and the winds mainly light, and, what with icebergs to marvel at and penguins to watch, this sail through the Scotia Sea would have been enjoyable enough but for the strained atmosphere on board and the daily scenes with Carreo. The Scotia Sea lies between South Georgia and the South Orkneys which were now about 150 miles to our south. It is named after the Norwegian steam whaler *Scotia* in which in 1903 the Scottish Antarctic expedition penetrated deep into the Weddell Sea and later wintered on Laurie Island in the South Orkneys. In default of home support, Bruce, the leader of the expedition, handed the Laurie Island base over to the Argentine Republic, thus providing a starting point for their claim to the sovereignty of the South Orkneys. In Lat. 59° S., for the first time for some weeks the air temperature rose above 40° F. and since by now we had written off the stove this small rise was the more welcome. The genoa, too, had had to be written off, having split badly. Instead we used one of the twin staysails, a sail that gave a lot more drive than the working jib but was too heavy to be of much use in light winds. On the 14th, as a reminder of where we were, a bitter south-east wind covered the deck with snow, and on the following night a moderate gale from the same quarter obliged us to heave to.

Although by now the nights were sufficiently dark we were disappointed not to see any aurora displays. On most nights the sky was anyway too cloudy and star sights were seldom obtainable. For working sights I had now to use the 1966 *Nautical Almanac*. I think I am right in saying that neither Brown's nor Reed's, the two Almanacs generally in use by yachtsmen, offer any help to the mariner who finds himself at sea with only an Almanac for the previous year, whereas the Almanac published by H.M. Nautical Almanac Office of the Royal Greenwich Observatory, containing nothing but the astronomical ephemeris, provides for this contingency with a simple rule which enables one to work out sun and star sights. It cannot be used for the moon or for planets. I am told that if you keep a Nautical Almanac for four years it again becomes current*, so that the thrifty navigator who has plied his trade for four consecutive years and has kept his Almanacs need never buy another.

---

*   I am also told on high authority, second only to that of the Astronomer Royal, that this four-year rule holds good only for the sun. Since most amateur

The Old Harbour, Bahia, Brazil, covered market on right

By January 20th I reckoned we were about a hundred miles off South Georgia. The penguins that we had heard mooing all night were, I hoped, natives of the island, and sure enough at ten next morning we sighted land. By evening we were off First Rock near the south-west corner in a freshening wind and snow squalls. When Carreo, in a violent squall, executed a Chinese gybe, I took the hint and hove-to. The night was dark and earlier we had sighted some small bergs. We had taken fifteen days, an average of seventy miles a day, whereas Shackleton in his ship's lifeboat, living in appalling conditions, had taken sixteen days. Elephant Island, whence he had started, is 150 miles nearer; on the other hand his *James Caird*'s sail area compared with *Mischief*'s must have been derisory. The fact that she went so fast is no doubt accounted for by the different weather in January and in May. In May 1915 the indomitable crew of the *James Caird* had suffered and at the same time benefitted from gales or near gales for most of the voyage.

Although it is 500 miles further north, South Georgia, particularly at its southern end, is in appearance almost as arctic as the South Shetlands. As has been noted already, the Antarctic convergence lies well to the north of the island. From a few miles off we could make out nothing but snow peaks, steep glaciers, and precipitous, black headlands. The island was discovered, or rediscovered, by Cook in 1775 on the first of his three great voyages. 'The wild rocks', he wrote, 'raised their lofty summits until they were lost in the clouds, and the valleys lay covered with everlasting snow. Not a tree was to be seen, nor a shrub even big enough to make a toothpick.' The name of Cape Disappointment at the southwestern corner of the island perhaps reflects his feelings upon seeing unbounded ocean to the south, convincing proof that he had discovered only an island and not a southern continent. 'The disappointment I now met with,' he says, 'did not affect me much; for to judge of the bulk by the sample it would not be worth the discovery.'

Sailing up the east coast next day we encountered a strong headwind and rather than stand out to sea to tack all night we anchored in Hound Bay, sixteen miles short of Grytviken, the Port of Entry for

---

navigators rely mainly upon sun sights, the value of this tip to the impecunious or parsimonious remains undiminished.

South Georgia. Except for the grunts and groans of numerous sea elephants the night passed quietly. Proceeding up the coast next day I
found the number of small inlets so confusing that we came to Right
Whale Rocks at the entrance to Cumberland Bay unexpectedly soon. A
small lighthouse stands on these rocks which are covered with tussock
grass. The day was sunny and serene, and the broad, calm expanse of
the bay with its grass-fringed shores and low surrounding hills might
have been likened to a Highland loch but for the great Nordenskjöld
glacier that filled the whole of its southern end. The two-mile wide and
seventy-foot high ice front of this magnificent glacier is lapped by the
sea and is constantly calving.

The bay appeared so empty and devoid of any trace of human
activity that we were puzzled as to the whereabouts of King Edward
Cove and the settlement. When we had sailed a few miles towards
the glacier the wind died, and as we handed the sails the narrow
entrance to the cove began to open out. On a rock bluff overlooking
the entrance, Hope Point, we could make out the white cross of the
Shackleton memorial. Shackleton, of course, did not make his landing here but at King Haakon Bay on the north-west side of the island.
Thence the three strongest men of the boat party made their extraordinary forced march of thirty-six hours over unknown mountainous
country, bemused often by fog, and without tent or sleeping bags, till
they arrived at the whaling station in Stromness Bay to the north of
Cumberland Bay. A whale catcher soon picked up the three men left at
King Haakon Bay, and in August after many setbacks, a Chilean vessel
with Shackleton on board rescued the twenty-two men marooned
on Elephant Island. The Boss, as his men called him, never let them
down. Shackleton (as a schoolboy before the First World War I once
heard him lecture) was a man whom nothing daunted, a man equal to
any emergency by sea or by land, but of this journey he wrote:

> When I look back at those days I do not doubt that Providence
> guided us, not only across those snowfields, but also across the
> stormy white sea which separated Elephant Island from our landing
> place on South Georgia. I know that during that long march of 36
> hours over the unnamed mountains and glaciers of South Georgia it
> often seemed to me that we were four, not three.

Soon the big whaling station at Grytviken and the small British settlement on King Edward Point came into view. Here the works of man do not obtrude too much upon the scene. For a man who likes his scenery stern and wild—provided he turns his back on the red roofs of the settlement—Grytviken is one of the loveliest harbours. The wooden, weather-worn buildings of the whaling station, the white church with its black steeple, nestle below snow-covered hills, while beyond, near enough for the details of their aspiring faces and ridge to be seen, tower two glorious mountains. Sugartop (7023 feet) and Mount Paget (9625 feet) are only two of the stronger and more monumental summits of many on the Allardyce Range which, together with the Salvesen Range, forms the island's formidably, rugged backbone. From it many icy, lofty ribs extend towards either coast. Here are the Alps in miniature, their attractions augumented by exotic fauna, sea views, and a total absence of huts and armies of climbers. Much has already been done there by expeditions but now that the shore whaling stations are closed the difficulties of transport are greatly increased. It becomes therefore an ideal objective for a man with a boat who is addicted to climbing, the more so because of the many beautiful fjords and safe anchorages that abound on the coasts of South Georgia.

A small crowd had assembled on the little wooden jetty at the settlement, where willing hands soon helped us to secure alongside. Here we had something like a welcome, the warmest and kindest that *Mischief* has anywhere enjoyed. A customs officer, delighted to have something to do, soon cleared us, the doctor came on board with kind enquiries, immediately followed by the administrative officer and his wife, Mr and Mrs Coleman. Within minutes an electric heater and electric light had been led into the cabin, and we were accorded the freedom of Shackleton House, a large two-storey building where the bachelors lived, where baths, beds, and meals would be provided. Mr Coleman, himself a retired sea captain, having arranged for a board for *Mischief* to ride against, then took me to his own house for a bath and a meal. Showers are no substitute for the real thing and I was in the mood to appreciate a bath, having been without since we left England. The beautifully fitted house, the warmth, carpets and easy chairs, compared very favourably with *Mischief*'s cabin.

Adjoining the living-room was a built-on conservatory where under Mrs Coleman's devoted care, geraniums, roses, fuschias, and other flowers flourished exceedingly. Nor can there be many, if any, other conservatories in the world whence you can look down upon families of sea elephants lying blissfully asleep in their mud wallows among tussock grass. Indeed, if you opened the conservatory windows you could smell them.

There were about a dozen people at the station including four married couples who had their own bungalows. All houses and offices were linked by telephone. The station had been established primarily to keep a check on the whaling operations, to attend to ships' business, and to maintain order among the shore staffs and the crews of the whaling ships. This was no sinecure. In 1958, for example, the population of the three whaling stations at Grytviken, Leith Harbour, and Stromness amounted in the summer to 1265, including seven women, and if the whaling fleet was in the number might be swollen to 3000. All shore-based whaling has now ceased, so that the only ships to call are relief ships on their way to or from the Antarctic. This news practically extinguished any hopes of getting rid of Carreo, but Mr Coleman agreed to send a signal to Port Stanley to ask if he could be put on board a relief ship due in about two months. I had a peaceful night alone on *Mischief*, the crew sleeping at Shackleton House where, I gathered, they had had a fairly riotous time.

The whaling station occupies the far end of the cove and is about half a mile from the station by a jeepable track. In winter when the snow lies deep one would have to go on foot on skis. Snow banks still lay by the track, and we were told that a former administrative officer had been killed by an avalanche when ski-ing along the track. Next day I walked over to the whaling station to meet the manager, an English-speaking Norwegian. In spite of a natural disgust for the slaughter of the harmless, majestic whale, I felt sad at seeing this remote, little town into which much money must have been poured, now almost dead—the huge flensing platforms, power plant, boiler rooms, workshops, barracks, clubhouse, football ground, church, the two forlorn whale catchers at the jetty, all deserted. On the other hand, had the brutal and bloody business of chopping up whales been in full swing one would no doubt have thought that the sooner it ended the better.

The manager's house, a fine, big building, comfortably furnished and brightly decorated, was still in use, though some of its windows were already being boarded up. In front on what in more genial climates would have been the lawn, stood a massive flagpole and a mounted harpoon gun, flanked by two enormous, old time trypots. A care and maintenance party of five men were busy about the place where a few years ago there would have been three hundred. Four of them were due to leave on the next relief ship, leaving a single caretaker who would live over at the British station. The manager having asked if we were in need of any stores, we made a tour of several well-stocked store-houses, including a refrigerated store, and got together a liberal collection which the manager undertook to ferry over in his boat. While over that side I visited the well-kept cemetery where Shackleton is buried. He died of a heart attack on board his ship *Quest* on January 5th, 1922, while off South Georgia.

From the sublime to the sordid and the ridiculous. Upon returning to *Mischief* I found Louis drunk and Carreo incapably drunk, kneeling on deck crooning quietly to himself. The binnacle had been badly bent by someone falling on it—happily the compass was all right—and the locker containing what remained of the ship's liquor bashed open with a hammer. On the table were two empty gin bottles and a half-empty bottle of cherry brandy. The latter must have been given them or stolen, but the two gin bottles were the last of our stock. Henceforth *Mischief* would perforce be a 'dry' ship. Leaving them I walked up to Shackleton House for lunch, pursued by desultory abuse from Louis, imploring me, amongst other things, to jump into the dock.

By evening Carreo was on his feet, roaming about in a maudlin state, and reported to be carrying a knife. Mr Coleman thought he should be locked up for the night, and having had in the recent past three whaling stations to look after he was fully qualified to handle drunks. Together with his henchman who acted as the local police force, he led Carreo unsuspectingly into a room with a bunk and turned the key on him. He did not appear to be carrying any knife. Later in the voyage Herbert, for reasons unknown, presented me with a signed statement concerning this incident. No statement signed by Herbert is of any value but it is worth inserting even if only on account of some curiosities of spelling:

For the Lookbook.

On the 26th January 1967, 20.15 hours at Gritiven, South Georgia, I went on board the yacht *Mischief* with Mr Vera the Chilean cook of the Shackleton House. The engineering officer Carreo Artigas was drunk on board and in possession of a knife. He said to me, 'I will kill the skipper when he returns from his visit to Mr Coleman's house.' I asked him to give me the knife and he repeated his threat to kill the skipper. I asked him again for the knife and he began to fight with me. Mr Vera was witness to all this. At 21.30 Mr Coleman arrested Carreo Artigas and put him in gail overnight. In my opinion Artigas althoogh drunk was responsible for his actions at that time.

By the following day we had a reply from Port Stanley concerning Carreo, firmly declining to help. He had sobered up and looked the worse for wear, slouching around in a blue greatcoat, his brown complexion, slightly mottled after his drinking bout, set off not to advantage by the crimson cap. He presented a new problem for us by firmly refusing to go to Cape Town. Mr Coleman, who had kindlier feelings towards him, talked to him like a father but failed to dissuade him or to convince him that he would get no passage in the next relief ship. Apparently versed in the tradition of resistance movements, albeit his was a private one, he talked of taking to the hills. Meantime the rest of the crew expressed their apprehension and their reluctance to sail with him. True, there was no longer any drink on board but they disliked the thought of Carreo awake on watch and them asleep below. As Macbeth said: 'Tis better thee without, than he within.'

Having brought the man there I had to take him away. Port Stanley in the Falklands, where Chileans and Uruguayans were said to be working on the roads, was only 900 miles away; but that had to be ruled out because it lay dead to windward. Quietness, according to the Chinese proverb, is worth buying. Realising that it was a devilish high price to pay, and sorely against the grain, I decided to deposit him where I got him. If he knew that we were bound for Montevideo we had some chance of peace on board, whereas if we ignored his violently expressed objections and sailed for Cape Town I felt that anything might happen, including his disappearance overboard. The others, while they saw the sense of this decision, were annoyed and bitterly disappointed at having to alter our plans on account of this wretched man. We had all looked forward to Cape Town and our mail awaited us there. I felt particularly exasperated. Friends were expecting me, I had counted on having the boat hauled out there, and the voyage homewards from Cape Town is quicker and far less troublesome than it is from Montevideo.

The news that we would return to Montevideo almost decided Herbert to start his resistance movement. Hours of brooding in the night watches had given his thoughts a new turn. No one, I believe, at Montevideo cared tuppence about this German ex-cyclist who now interviewed Mr Coleman in his office and solemnly demanded 'political asylum'. Nothing less than his life was at stake, for if he returned to Montevideo it would be in danger! Incidentally Herbert's disease which had baffled the combined wisdom of the Chilean and Argentine medical staff had been swiftly diagnosed and successfully treated by Dr Parker—scabies. On learning this we took care to keep Herbert well clear of the galley.

Throughout our stay none of the crew showed up on board. In spite of orders from Mr Coleman that they were no longer to sleep there they continued to eat and sleep at Shackleton House. With the help of the engineer who ran the power plant I got the boat watered and stocked up with diesel oil and paraffin. He also fixed up a winch and persuaded the galley pump to work, and, the Norwegians having brought the promised stores, we were ready to leave. Except for one day when snow had fallen the weather had been remarkably pleasant, notwithstanding the moans of the oldest inhabitants about the wretched summer. But for the paramount desire I had to get on with the voyage and to see the last of the crew, I should have enjoyed an excursion to the Nordenskjöld glacier, or to Cumberland West Bay where, we were told, reindeer could be seen.

But before we got safely away one more curious incident gave me food for thought. I appointed the morning of Saturday, January 28th for our departure, reserving some doubts as to whether the appointment would be kept. On the Friday night I dined at the Coleman's with the doctor and one or two others. About 11 p.m. the telephone rang. Mike was at the other end and here was an occasion when he recognised his duty towards me and the ship and practised it. Speaking very guardedly he said that during the evening there had been some 'wild talk' and that I had better get back on board. Walking down to the jetty I could see that though no light was on somebody was on board with a torch. Tom and Herbert were standing in the galley. Herbert's wits were nimble enough to have offered some plausible explanation, but without answering any questions they went up the companionway and walked off into the night. With Mr Coleman I hung about for a bit and then I turned in and read until daylight. Following hard upon Mike's warning this midnight visit looked suspicious. A forced stay or delay at South Georgia might have suited some of the crew. But this is conjecture, as conjectural as the number of battalions there were in a Chinese horde.

Having made all secure on deck preparatory to sailing I watched the kind people of the station assembling to see us go, and then to my relief the crew came on board. Having made our farewells we cast off in drizzling rain and a flat calm.

CHAPTER X

MONTEVIDEO AND HOMEWARDS

M ONTEVIDEO LIES ABOUT 1700 MILES north-west of South Georgia, a distance that we might have run in about three weeks; but until we were clear of the Westerlies and in the region of variable winds we could not expect often to lay the required course. In fact we logged 2000 miles and took four weeks. With the wind hanging in the north, and light at that, three days had elapsed before we were clear of South Georgia. At least I hoped we were clear, for the radio receiver had packed up and we could get no time signals. Carreo diagnosed a fault in the condenser so I resigned myself to doing without time signals until we reached Montevideo. According to the Taoist doctrine—and it sounds very sensible—if you practise inaction nothing will be left undone. As practised on this occasion it worked like a charm. We did nothing, and in a few days the wireless came on again as suddenly as it had gone off.

On February 1st we suffered a minor calamity for which I was entirely to blame. When the barometer fell to 28.6 we expected something in the way of wind. Nothing happened until the barometer started to rise about midnight when we had to reef down and heave to, the wind blowing with some violence from dead ahead. At 4 a.m. a small tear appeared in the leach of the mainsail just above the reef, but as the wind had backed and moderated we started sailing. This kept the sail quiet. Two hours later, in my watch, the tear had not increased and I reckoned it would hold until the crew turned out for breakfast when we could lower the sail. Then the wind suddenly dropped, the boom started kicking, the leach rope broke, and before one could say 'Jack', let alone 'Jack Robinson', the sail ripped right across from leech to luff, all twenty-four feet of it. Moreover it was not a seam that had gone, but a tear in the cloth, a jagged tear. When the sea had gone down a bit we got the spare mainsail up and bent on. The spare sail had been very tightly folded, nevertheless we had a mighty struggle to get it through the cabin door. As the torn sail could not be mended properly at sea, and as there was no hope of stowing it below, we had to lash it on deck. At Montevideo we could take it ashore and make a job of it.

The spare sail, an older sail and thin in places, had to be carefully watched. At the least sign of a seam going we had it down for repair and in hard blows we set the trysail. The early hours of the following morning were equally eventful. Carreo had the 4 a.m. to 6 a.m. watch and the wind and incessant rain may have given him an added touch of gall. When Herbert came up to relieve him they at once fell to exchanging blows in the cockpit, the appropriate place for two such birds to fight. But *Mischief* sailed placidly on giving me time to intervene. Half an hour later, when Herbert had brought off a smart Chinese gybe and I went up again to assess the damage, the rain had turned to snow. The weather soon mended, we put in a good day's run, and that night we recrossed the Antarctic convergence. The sea temperature went up from 37° to 45° F.

On February 6th a full gale at north-west set in. By nightfall we set the trysail and jogged along all night heading east of north, a direction which provoked a wild outburst from Carreo. Those who know little suspect the most. In spite of the daily positions marked on the chart for all to see he remained unconvinced that we were not bound for Cape Town. If only we had been bound there these predominant north-westerly winds would have given us a rare lift. Instead we had always a fight to gain any westing.

At last in anti-cyclone conditions we enjoyed a fair wind at south-west and in four days logged 430 miles, all in the right direction. A small school of killer whales swam around for several hours. Even at a distance these tigers of the sea are easily distinguished by the long, narrow dorsal fin standing three or four feet above the water. These were close enough for us to see also the characteristic white mark abaft the eye and their white bellies. In Lat. 45° S. the sea temperature had risen to 53° F. and the next day, February 17th, it rose to 62° F, whereupon we shed our woolly garments and I had a bucket bath. This was evidently the sub-tropical convergence, the transition from sub-antarctic water to what is known as the Central Water Mass. The winds pay no heed to convergence; they continued extremely variable, from near gales to flat calms or dirty rain-laden squalls. Reefing and unreefing, nursing the slightly delicate spare mainsail, kept us alert and occupied.

By February 15th the light green colour of the water warned us that we were in soundings and by next day we were crossing the great estuary of the Plate, neither land nor ships anywhere in sight. The water turned yellow and looked so alarmingly shallow that one expected every minute to feel the keel grate on the sandy bottom. A sounding gave us two fathoms. We were on the English Bank, an extensive shoal south of Montevideo, where in places there is not enough water to float *Mischief*, and where the buoys that are supposed to define its limits have always eluded us. It was gratifying when the high buildings of Montevideo, shimmering like a mirage, at last came up dead ahead, and I could not refrain from giving Carreo a final jolt by telling him that we had arrived at Cape Town. At one time I had thought of going instead to Buenos Aires, a hundred miles up the river, where there might be less difficulty in finding the two or three hands that would be needed to get us home. There are many more yacht clubs there, for the Argentinians are more boat-minded, or perhaps richer, than the Uruguayans. As events soon showed, Buenos Aires would have been a serious mistake.

There being no mooring buoy available at Puerto Buceo we had to anchor. Carreo and Louis departed that evening, unregretted, followed next day by Tom and Mike. Tom I had expected would go, for he now looked upon me as a man who had deceived him by issuing a false prospectus, persuading him to invest time—happily no money—in a South Sea Bubble. Mike's departure surprised me for the second and what I imagined would surely be the last time. After so many arduous days at sea he thought it preposterous that I should hope to sail within a week, and that he should be immediately asked to help get the torn mainsail on shore was quite outrageous. Both he and Tom made themselves at home with some Uruguayans living on board their boat moored at the club jetty.

This speedy reduction of the crew to one was not so serious a blow as another that fell upon me the same day. A man can go nowhere without money, as the Bulgarians say, not even to church. I now discovered that an unused book of travellers cheques for a large amount had disappeared. Naturally, and probably wrongly, Carreo came under suspicion. Herbert assured me that he had taken and flogged them at Punta Arenas where there was reputedly a market for such things. When Carreo returned to collect his gear he denied any knowledge of the cheques. By rummaging the ship I collected some working capital, five pesos, enough for the bus fare into the city, the fare, by the way, having doubled since our last visit. What a good thing it was that we had not gone to Buenos Aires where I should have been right up the creek. At Maclean and Stapledon's, the shipping agents, I could rely upon aid and comfort; upon Mr Maclean for cash and upon his able assistant Mr McClew for comfort. Having cashed a sterling cheque for £100 I returned to the boat with this amount in thousand-peso notes. Herbert and I were now living alone on board. He had always appeared to me honest in money matters, but I waited until he was out of the cabin before putting this cash away in a place where it was not likely to be found by pickers-up of unconsidered trifles.

After a severe struggle Herbert and I got the torn mainsail on shore and spread out on the Club lawn where I spent the next week pleasantly enough sitting in the sun plying the needle, first herring-boning the whole thing together and then covering the tear with long strips of nine-inch wide canvas. Soon I had an able assistant in a Mr Hills, almost a professional sailmaker, who took on the job of repairing the working jib which was also in a bad way. He had been at sea for many years around the Falkland Islands and had a son who was second engineer in the *Darwin*, a small ship, the only ship, that plies regularly between Montevideo and Port Stanley. Mr Hills and I had met at the Sailor's Home, the fountain source of some of our troubles, where he had been to see his friend the Major. I had no intention of tapping that source again, my visit was merely to retail our experiences to the Major, and to tell him, in sorrow rather than anger, how his swan Carreo had turned out an ill-favoured duck.

This time, for a free trip direct to England instead of via the Antarctic, I anticipated less difficulty in finding a crew; but at the various shipping agents and consulates I had no more success than before. I had struck up an acquaintance with a Swede, an ex-sea captain who lived alone on his small motor boat moored by the sea wall. He was a convivial soul with an interminable swallow so far as whisky was concerned; a man who, like the rest of us, had had his troubles and possibly deserved them. Cigarettes and other dutiable articles thrown overboard from passing steamers and picked up by a motor boat that happened to be around, found a ready sale in Montevideo. But all good things must come to an end. After his boat had been confiscated my Swedish friend had luckily been able to buy it back, but now it was not allowed to leave the harbour. To come to the point, the Swede had in his employ a Uruguayan lad, Roberto, who had an urge to travel. He had been a fisherman, was cheerful, willing, capable, and a good cook. The Swede spoke highly of him and encouraged me to take him on. Roberto had to get a passport, and judging from the dilatory habits of officials the world over, I thought this might take three weeks. To the credit of Uruguay he had it in three days.

So we were now three, for I assumed that Herbert's desire to revisit the Fatherland was unabated. He had learnt no sea sense, and never would, but he remained always cheerful, and I had come to regard him as a part of *Mischief*, a part that should not be leant upon too heavily. One day, while I worked on the sail, Mike came by. We exchanged a few words, words became an argument, and the argument grew heated. In reviling it is not necessary to prepare a preliminary draft. By the time I had said my piece I did not expect that he would want to talk to me again, but about a week later I learnt from Mr McClew, in whom both Tom and Mike confided that he wanted to rejoin. Well inured now to Mike's vagaries, I agreed. He did some work on board, including overhauling the charging engine, but continued to live with his friends in the other boat until the last possible minute.

At about this stage I had a cable from a friend in England asking if I would take on a lad of eighteen who had just left Pangbourne*, and was desperately keen to make a voyage. Nor was he deterred when I suggested that an air passage to Montevideo would be a high price to pay for what would inevitably be a rather humdrum voyage. No sea voyage can be dull for a man who has an eye for the ever-changing sea and sky, the waves, the wind, and the way of a ship upon the water; but in tropic seas there is not much else to look at and the weather is unlikely to provide a challenge for an ardent young sailor. More cables passed and in the end young Robin arrived on March 19th at the airport

---

*   At this time, a school for intending Merchant Navy officers—Ed

where Roberto and I met him. We were due to sail in two days so he had little time in which to see Montevideo. Happily that was not part of his programme; his sole wish was to buy a gaucho's hat. Gauchos are not a monopoly of the Argentine, Uruguay has them, too, and the necessary pampas on which to deploy them. But Robin had no luck, either the shops were shut for a fiesta, or the gauchos, like everyone else, have stopped wearing hats. He had to content himself with an apparatus for drinking *yerba maté*—very much cheaper, I believe, than hats.

But I am anticipating events. Herbert and I continued to live placidly on board until March 10th. In the mornings he did the necessary shopping and in the afternoon went into the city whence he usually got back about 11 p.m. He had apparently forgotten that in Montevideo his freedom or even his life might be in danger; or perhaps his political enemies were no longer in power, for there had recently been an election and a new President reigned. Herbert had little or no money so I was naturally curious about how he paid his way on these visits. He told me he spent the time at the Cyclists club where old friends or rivals reminisced about long days in the saddle. I felt tempted to join him and thought I would qualify, having once spent some very long days in the saddle when riding a pushbike from Kenya to the Cameroons.

Anchored in Puerto Buceo one never felt quite at ease. Even in summer hard blows from south-west, the 'pamperos', and from southeast, the 'sudestada', are by no means infrequent. In the mornings there might be no one on board *Mischief*, or perhaps Herbert alone, who by himself could not even have started the engine. On the night of the 10th it began blowing very hard from south-west. By midnight, which was unusual, Herbert had not returned. I passed an anxious night, going on deck at frequent intervals to see if we were dragging. Early in the morning we began to move slowly but surely stern first towards the inner breakwater, a jumble of huge concrete blocks. Alone, there was little I could do except stand by with the engine going, but when we were a short fifty yards from what looked like destruction the anchor somehow took a fresh hold and held us there steadfastly.

When Herbert had not returned I began to think he might have had grounds for his fears, or perhaps he had been roughed up by thugs as had happened to him before. On the third day I bought a newspaper to see if any body had been fished out of the river, as bodies frequently

The British station at King Edward Point, from the cemetery at Grytviken, South Georgia

were. A body had been found but it was not Herbert. There were a few of his belongings in his bunk but his cherished package of newspaper cuttings were missing—an ominous sign. On the fourth day after his disappearance I had occasion to open up what I fondly imagined to be the secret cache and found it empty. Herbert had vamoosed with 18,000 pesos, about £90, and no doubt with my travellers cheques, too, for what they were worth. For him at any rate the voyage had not been unfruitful. As a matter of form, for Herbert had four days' start, I informed the police who were not altogether surprised. From the water-guard at Buceo I learnt that prior to his departure he had been enquiring about the bus service to Brazil. This may have been a blind— he was a wily bird—and he might easily have gone to Buenos Aires. The German consul who had been so relieved when I took Herbert away, learnt with sorrow that he was again at large in South America. He would have to reopen the Bittner file. Once more penniless I again had recourse to Mr MacLean. I thought it advisable to lower my sights. The £40 he let me have would have to see us through.

Our number was again reduced to four and I might well have left it at that. We had made long passages before with that number but a three-months voyage with only three watchkeepers is hard work. With some misgivings I put an advertisement in one of the newspapers and the consequent flood of applicants reached alarming proportions. At least sixty came on the first day and not many fewer on the next. With the help of my Swedish friend we soon weeded them out. It was not a matter of asking whether a man had any sea experience, the important point was whether they had a passport and some money. Already having Roberto on my hands I did not want to bring to England another Uruguayan whose fare home, if the worst came to the worst, might be my liability. Few of them had passports, fewer still had any money, and only about two of them had both. The young Italian student, Sergio, whom I finally took on looked a bit of a 'cissy' but spoke excellent English as well as Spanish and Italian. He could interpret to the non-English speaking Roberto and would be company for him. He proved a most regrettable choice but at that stage of the voyage it hardly mattered.

We were about ready to go. The stores that I could afford came on board and I noted with dismay how little cash remained to spend at the Azores, our next stop. We had no need to go alongside for water,

enough having been ferried off by Herbert and I in the course of our
long stay. Roberto's local knowledge came in useful for he readily
found a baker who prepared for us about 70 lb of 'tostada', a thing
that the ship chandlers had never been able to do. With the essential
help of Mr McClew we got our clearance; by noon of March 21st all
were on board, and having got our anchors (we now had two down)
we sailed out.

This passage from Montevideo to the Azores in which we logged
6260 miles took eighty-six days, an average of seventy-three miles
a day. This is the longest that *Mischief* has been at sea, her previous
record being seventy-four days between the Canaries and Cape Town.
Had we started this homeward run from Cape Town, as originally
intended, we should have had the southeast Trades behind us almost
from the first day. Starting from Montevideo, before we could hope to
pick up the Trades, we had to make about 1500 miles to the north-east
which at this time of year, the southern autumn, is precisely the direction of the prevailing winds. In addition there is a south-going current.
At times, when progress seemed pitifully slow, I feared we might have
to put into Recife for food, if not for water. Water was no problem. So
heavy and frequent were the storms of rain that we crossed the equator, forty-nine days out, with all tanks and containers full. It cost us
thirty days' sailing to reach the region of the Trades, and then, instead
of carrying us 2° or 3° north of the equator as they should have done,
they petered out in Lat. 3° S. But that is all part of the game. The wind
bloweth where it listeth, and those whose pleasure lies in making use
of the wind must make the best of it.

Our modest rate of progress may have been the reason why we
caught some fish on this long passage. One reads with envy of raft voyages such as *Kon Tiki*, or of Dr Bombard in his rubber dinghy, and the
number of fish that daily gathered round asking to be caught. On days
when our progress was raft-like we usually had numbers of dorado
in attendance. The barnacles and lush vegetation that by now decorated our hull attracted schools of small fish that swam tirelessly just
ahead of the stem or lurked under the keel, darting away at intervals
to inspect some choice morsel. The Sargasso weed, too, that drifted
by, provided these hungry little beggars with plenty of small crabs and
shrimps. At first we despised their small size, nor did they appear likely

to be caught, but after long perseverance Mike found a way. The record for one day was seventeen. Besides the small fry there were others of 1 lb to 2 lb in weight of which we caught several. These had tiny but exceedingly powerful mouths which they used, we were pleased to see, for wrenching barnacles off the hull. One always associates crabs with the foreshore and it seemed strange to find crabs that measured three inches across in mid-ocean. The small crabs found on the weed were fierce cannibals; if several of them were together in a bucket of water they tore each other to pieces.

The flying fish needed no catching and often provided our lunch. All was grist that came to our mill including the commonly despised garfish—all snout and tail, green bones, but perfectly edible. The dorado were too smart for us; we got only one which Roberto killed with a superb shot from his home-made harpoon; the handle of our broom tipped with the cunningly filed leg of a Primus stove. This dorado, with lovely iridescent green and gold colouring, was about three feet long. Twice Roberto hit a shark with this harpoon. The shark appeared soon after we had all been bathing over the side and although only some five feet long caused as much alarm as if he had been twenty feet long. It soon rid itself of the harpoon but reappeared a week later; at least we were convinced that this was the same shark by a white scar on its back just where the harpoon had hit. This second time Roberto lodged the harpoon in his head whence it did not draw until after some wild threshing and the running out of all the line.

Before we reached the Azores we were glad to eke out our food stocks with fish. We were low on bully beef and right out of cheese, jam, and butter. Our twice-baked bread had lasted for sixty-four days and I reckoned it would have lasted another week had it not been for Sergio. No one but him ate bread at supper, the big meal of the day, and this extravagant habit had always been frowned upon. Frowns were wasted upon Sergio, whose self-esteem rendered him impervious to criticism. Italians are gluttons for carbohydrates, flour in all shapes and forms, but no Italian that I knew—and I have lived with some hungry Italian hordes—could hold a candle to Sergio. And he took his time over it. Compared with Sergio, Gladstone who chewed each mouthful thirty-two times, merely gobbled. The first man to finish his meal usually relieved the helmsman, a custom that inevitably absolved

Sergio from this duty. Having relieved the helmsman, and having in turn been relieved by him when he had finished his meal, one would go below to find Sergio still calmly hoisting it in. Though intelligent enough, he never tried to learn, and when we reached Lymington he no more knew which rope was which than on the day he embarked. So much did he grate on me that I looked forward to the day of our arrival mainly because it would signify, I hoped, Sergio's departure. When, therefore, six weeks later I returned to Lymington and found him, unasked, still living on board I felt as Macbeth felt when he heard that Fleance, whose death he had confidently expected, still lived: 'Then comes my fit again.' Normally I am not much worried by my cabin companions however odd their behaviour, but evidently at this stage of a trying voyage my dislike for this harmless Italian youth had become morbid. So long as he does not go to sea and avoids jobs that involve hurrying over his meals, I imagine, I might even hope, that Sergio will do well.

Few of us are without one redeeming feature. Sergio did his stint in the galley in turn with Mike and Roberto and did it very well. Robin took so long to learn how to light a Primus that we were unwilling to suffer while he learnt how to cook. In him I sustained another disap-pointment, having looked forward to having on board for a change an eager, willing, cadet-type, the first to reach the deck when called and the last to leave, foremost when any work involving dirt or difficulty needed doing. With Mike, Roberto and Sergio vying with each other, we had some delectable and exotic meals. Roberto had brought with him a round oven to sit on top of a Primus, thus enabling us to have syrup tarts, soda bread, toad-in-the-hole, *canalones*, Cornish pasties, and cottage pies.

We met few ships. A Russian tanker altered course from about five miles away to pass close along our lee side, dipped his ensign, and gave us three blasts on the whistle; and the *Aragon* of the Royal Mail line also closed us to let her passengers take photographs. We suspected that the Russians had heard vaguely of Sir Francis Chichester, who was in the South Atlantic at that time, and had paid us these marks of respect in mistake, though few things could be more difficult, one imagines, than to mistake *Mischief* for *Gypsy Moth*, either in appear-ance or performance. We met the north-east Trades when we were due south of the Azores in Long. 30° W. and consequently, before we had run through the Trades, sailing close-hauled all the time, we had been pushed as far west as Long. 41°. Being then, in theory, in the region of the Westerlies, we were able to steer more or less towards the Azores. As we were approaching the islands from a little south of west the nearest port of entry for us was Horta on Fayal, the other possible port, San Miguel, lying one hundred miles further east. We were in the grip of the Azores 'high' with very light winds, so that a hundred miles meant for us a matter of days. At Montevideo, undecided as to which particular island we should fetch, and since England would then be only three weeks away, I had advised the crew not to have mail sent to the Azores. They now told me they were all expecting mail at San Miguel.

At midday of June 15th we sighted the high ground on Fayal distant about twenty miles. We were surprised that the neighbouring island of Pico and its 7000-foot summit had not shown up long before. In the late afternoon this summit did manage to poke its head above the cloud but the rest of Pico might as well not have existed. Following in the wake of a small tunnyman we were met at the harbour entrance by the Pilot who took us to a convenient buoy. When we were secured, the Pilot entered and cleared us and we were free to land—no Customs, no police, no fuss. Would it were ever thus. Five other yachts lay in the harbour, two of them single-handers. At Horta, the *Café Sport*, presided over by the ever friendly and helpful Peter, is, in spite of its name, the Mecca for all visiting yachtsmen. Their comings and goings are all faithfully recorded in Peter's log-book. We had missed meeting the Hiscocks by two days and we sailed before the arrival of Dr David Lewis and his family in Rehu Moana, whom I had much hoped to see.

Horta is a delightful little town, beautifully kept by people who take pride in its appearance—flowers, shady trees and seats everywhere, speckless, tesselated pavements in black and white, a whitewashed sea wall, brass ringbolts in the quay, brightly coloured houses, wine good and cheap, friendly people, few motor cars, no bearded weirdies, television aerials, fun fairs, or juke boxes. A paradise, in fact, for squares.

Pleasant though all this was after so long at sea I was impatient to get on and to write *finis* to an unlucky voyage. So that it was with reluctance that I waited for five days until a boat from San Miguel arrived with the crew's mail. Mike ran true to form till the last. Although at this stage it was hardly worth while going through the motions of deserting for the third time, yet in order to make sure that we waited for the mail, he and Sergio left the boat. When the mail arrived on the evening of June 20th these worthies refused to come off until after midnight. The strong temptation to sail without them had to be resisted; the Portuguese would not like it, and we should probably have been pursued next morning by the Pilot's launch, a journey for which I might have had to pay. When Robin finally brought them off in the dinghy all three went below, shut the cabin door, and turned in. From now on, Mike said, they were going to please themselves rather than me, thus proclaiming a sort of seamen's strike, or merely working to rule. So Roberto and I hoisted in the dinghy, let go from the buoy, and motored out. Outside the harbour we hoisted sail and shared the watch on deck until the ineffable Mike appeared to take the 6 a.m. to 8 a.m. watch.

From the Azores to the Channel is about 1200 miles. Afflicted by light perverse winds, or no wind at all, we logged 1500 miles in twenty-five days, making in fact the slowest leg of the whole voyage. When we ran 300 miles in the first three days we thought we were almost home. Thereafter we only once exceeded one hundred miles and on one day we logged fifteen miles and on another twenty miles. The familiar, brightly painted tunny boats soon made their appearance, the first when we were nearly 500 miles west of Finisterre. They were catching tunny all right and, presently, to our infinite surprise, we had one, too, a fish of about 25 lb. This was the one and only fish to be caught on the line that we had trailed over the stern for the greater part of the voyage. All kinds of lures had been tried, white rags, red rags, shiny bits of tin, even a dead flying fish. When we caught this one we were sailing through frequent patches of discoloured water, so red that they might have been caused by the slaughter of several whales. In fact the discolouration was due to myriads of small shrimps. At Horta, the local boats fishing round the islands daily brought in catches of more than a hundred tunny of 40 to 50 lb weight.

The Azores 'high' followed us northwards. Fine, hazy weather with light easterly and north-easterly winds prevailed right across the

Bay of Biscay. Sailing on the port tack we failed to clear Ushant and made a lubberly sort of landfall to the south of it. Haze concealed the land but the presence of three French warships at exercise showed that we were off Brest. In the haze a radar scanner mounted on top of a funnel looked so like a tower that we mistook it at first for the Armen lighthouse. At night, when the lights came on, we saw this light to the south, Ushant to the north, and St Mathieu to the east. In settled summer weather the yachtsman might guess when he was in the Channel either by running into fog or by the number of racing pigeons that settle on his boat to cadge a lift. We emerged from the fog without being frightened by any steamers, and before we were off the Needles the last of our passengers had flown, though not without leaving their abundant traces behind.

On July 15th, a year and a day since our departure, we motored up Lymington River, having first cleared the Customs at Yarmouth. A nimble friend, who spotted us in the river, reached and warned the Yacht Club in time for them to give us their usual welcome of a one-gun salute. Two days later *Mischief* had been stripped bare and made ready for a long rest in her mud berth. She was none the worse for her experiences. As Conrad's shell-back, old Singleton exclaimed: 'Ships are all right. It's the men in them.' My relief at having arrived was more heartfelt than it normally is. More than once, at Deception Island and South Georgia, I had wondered when, if ever, *Mischief* would return home.

As the reader may have gathered, this 21,000-mile voyage had not furnished the enjoyment that is desirable and is expected on such voyages. Nor had it resulted in any achievement. We had nothing to show for it except the fact that the Antarctic, or the least hostile part of it, can readily be reached in a small boat. A voyage like this naturally entails the endurance of small privations and wearisome duties, and obviously all were not up to it. A man, however, must do his work with the tools provided, and if he himself provides the tools and finds them unsuitable, then so much the worse for him. On the other hand when we sail the seas we expect to be confronted with difficulties—that is one reason for doing it—so perhaps with a crew of thorough seamen and agreeable, staunch companions everything would have been too easy. But to have four misfits in a crew of five is too many.

PART TWO

Round Africa

June 1957–July 1958

Map 3: Track chart for Round Africa expedition

CHAPTER XI

THE START

———◆———

A N ACCOUNT OF A VOYAGE that took place ten years ago may seem dangerously like the writer's reminiscences. A man's experiences are said to be the name he gives to his mistakes, and his reminiscences are often written when his mistakes have been forgotten. It has been a bad habit of mine generally to write an account of journeys made by land or by sea. From the start the task was not easy and practice has made writing no easier, which is one good reason, coupled with the need for filling the winter evenings, why the habit is kept up. The reason that no account of this voyage came to be written was that I did not feel equal to it: not that the voyage was such an epic that no account could do it justice, but that I did not feel strong enough. As I still have the brief diary and the log-book of this voyage the following account is factual and not vaguely reminiscent.

Making a voyage round Africa had never been the intention. It resulted from trying to save something from the wreck of our hopes, hopes that had centred upon reaching the Crozet Islands, an enterprise of far more pith and moment than a circumnavigation of Africa. At this time, the autumn of 1956, *Mischief* was back from the voyage to the Patagonian channels and home by the west coast of South America and the Panama Canal, a voyage made solely for the purpose of landing a climbing party in the most favourable place from which to make a crossing of the Patagonian ice-cap.* With this first venture accomplished I felt satisfied that the apparently conflicting aims of sailing and climbing could be happily married, and that point being settled I began to look for a fresh venture.

Three likely objectives suggested themselves. The most ambitious was Heard Island, in Lat. 53° S., some 2500 miles south-east of Cape Town, a small island that is really one big mountain, 9000 feet

---

*   See *Mischief in Patagonia*, London, 1957.

high and draped in ice and snow from sea to summit. But there was
no secure anchorage; the boat having landed its climbing party would
have to be sailed to the much larger island of Kerguelen, 300 miles
more or less to windward in stormy latitudes. Moreover the crew faced
with this task would be weak, having been depleted by the landing of
the climbing party that necessarily included the climbing skipper.

Deciding that this was not on I turned to Kerguelen, a big island
abounding in good anchorages, its western end extremely mountainous. Kerguelen belongs to France, and some 700 miles to the west in
Lat. 47° S. is another small group of French islands, Îles Crozet, com-
prising five scattered islands, Île aux Cochons, Île de la Possession, Île
de l'Est, Îles des Apotres, and Îles des Pingouins, the last two being
mere clusters of rock pinnacles. They were discovered in the same year
as Kerguelen, 1772, by the French navigator Marion-Dufresne, who also
discovered what are now Marion and Prince Edward Islands. After the
murder of Dufresne in New Zealand, his second-in-command, Crozet,
took command of the expedition and his name was subsequently
applied to the whole group by Captain Cook. Like Kerguelen and
Heard Island, the Crozet were the haunt of British and American sealers during the first half of the nineteenth century until all the seals had
been pretty well exterminated. A few scientific expeditions on their
way to or from the Antarctic had paid brief visits to the islands, but
only the crews of ships that had been wrecked there made any prolonged sojourn. The survivors of the wreck of the *Strathmore* had the
worst time for she was wrecked on the Apostles, the least hospitable
island of all. The story is worth relating.

In the days of sail, ships bound for Australia or New Zealand ran
their easting down in the Roaring Forties. Hard driving masters with
a reputation for fast passages to maintain, or bent on establishing one,
might go as far south as the Fifties in the hope of finding stronger
or more prolonged gales. Thus in those days the Crozet were often
sighted by ships. The *Strathmore*, a new full-rigged ship from Dundee,
was running her easting down along the forty-seventh parallel in the
southern winter of 1875. Owing to thick weather no sights had been
obtained for several days and the master intended to check his position
and his chronometers by sighting the Crozet. Sail had been reduced so
as not to overrun the islands in the dark, but at midnight of July 1st the

vessel struck one of the rock islets of the Apostles. A gig and a lifeboat reached the shore and in the next two days ferried ashore those still clinging to the rigging and salvaged some valuable odds and ends—cooking pots, a case of spirits, blankets, a cleaver, and some buckets. A whole gale then blew up and smashed to pieces both boats. For six months, huddled in a rudely contrived shelter, the castaways eked out a wretched existence by eating albatross, mollymawks, and their eggs. Driftwood from the wreck enabled them to maintain a fire. To add to their distress they sighted two ships but failed to attract their attention. Finally in January 1876, forty-three men and one woman were taken off by an American whaler. Four had died on the island from their privations and forty, including the master and mate, had perished with the ship. A striking illustration of the difference modern means of communication make to the perils of the sea and the chances of rescue, is that ten months after the *Strathmore*'s survivors had been picked up H.M.S. *Wolverine* called at the Crozet in search of them.

Even in 1957 the Crozet were little known. The *Antarctic Pilot* of that date described Possession Island, the largest of the group, as having snow-covered mountains of about 5000 feet. This piece of erroneous information and the fact that they were little known weighed in their favour if it came to making a choice between Kerguelen and the Crozet. The high and rugged western half of Kerguelen, too, was little known; the ice-cap named Glacier Cook had never been trodden; Mount Ross (6430 feet) together with several lesser peaks had never been climbed. The many secure anchorages were an attraction, as was the presence of a French scientific base where help and local knowledge would no doubt be at our disposal. On the other hand there was no denying that the presence of other human beings did to a large extent detract from the glamour. The word 'uninhabited' on a map casts a spell almost as powerful as the word 'unexplored', and the lure of a remote, uninhabited island is hardly to be withstood.

Thus when we sailed in 1957 the Crozet were the main target. I might as well add here that when we succeeded in reaching them at the second attempt we were disappointed only by the mountains. Instead of 5000 feet they proved to be only 3000 feet high and their snow cover was not permanent. We were only just in time. A year or so later a French official expedition surveyed Possession Island and established a scientific base near the bay where we had landed. A téléférique now runs from the beach to the base above suspended over the large rookery of King penguins. The penguins may not care but any desire of mine to revisit Île de la Possession has been greatly lessened. I am glad to say that on the French map there is a Mont du Mischief, a tribute to a valiant and much enduring old boat.

In 1957 when *Mischief*'s voyages were little known I had few applicants and consequently some difficulty in finding crew. I have no record and do not remember how I collected the crew for this voyage, but I do not think I resorted to advertising as I did for the later more successful voyage. For that I had to put an advertisement in the Personal Column of *The Times*: 'Hand(man) wanted for long voyage in small boat. No pay, no prospects, not much pleasure.' I remember, however, that Mike Clay applied for a place when I gave a lecture at Cambridge where he was studying geography. He was a climber not a sailor. Jim Lovegrove, who lived in the same county as I did, must have been listening to the Welsh jungle drums. He was an artist who could turn his hand to many things, including wood carving. He carved a very handsome name-board for *Mischief*'s counter. Having had some experience in Thames sailing barges he knew how to handle heavy gear. I was a bit dubious about taking him, and indeed felt like a wrecker of homes, because he was a married man with a small infant and another on the way. As we were to be away a year I thought it pretty callous both on his part and mine.

How Gerry Levick heard of the enterprise I cannot imagine. He was an engineer working for a firm in Lancashire and I believe our first contact was by telephone when I was already at Lymington fitting out. He quickly gave himself the sack for the sake of making the voyage. No doubt he had sea fever, probably incurable, for since then he has been many years in the Mediterranean as professional skipper in various craft. Finally I got hold of two South Africans—this too must have been sheer accident—Pat Green and Howard Davies, both young, active, likely lads. The former, an experienced hand who had done a lot of sailing, was a valuable acquisition. Howard had no sea experience but bravely volunteered to cook and proved to be the better bargain of the two. I made it clear that in return for a free passage I expected them to complete the voyage to the Crozet and to disembark in South Africa only when we had returned from the islands. To which they agreed.

At that time *Mischief* carried her topmast, giving us the benefit of setting a topsail, and herself a proud, yachtlike appearance. The genoa halyard also went to the topmast head but even without the topmast we can set a genoa of much the same size. Whether or not the topsail gave her any more speed, the first leg to Las Palmas took sixteen days, exactly the same as on all the other occasions. Sailing from Lymington on June 30th, 1957, by 2 p.m. we were off the Needles where, with Mike Clay trying his 'prentice hand at the tiller, *Mischief* bounced smartly off the Bridge buoy, the ebb tide running strongly. It was strange and most appropriate, since Jim Lovegrove was on board, that in the Channel we met a Will Everard sailing barge. We have always been lucky in the Bay, lucky from the point of view of the 'fair one' in the following verse, not the hard-bitten 'snoring breeze' chap:

> Oh, for a fair and gentle breeze:
> I heard a fair one say,
> But give to me the snoring breeze
> And white waves leaping high.

We had calms and light airs all the way across until we picked up a fresh northerly breeze seventy miles north of Finisterre.

When we met the north-east Trades and set the twin staysails, which we did about July 9th, *Mischief* took the bit in her teeth and logged an average of 120 miles for the rest of the way. One night when we were doing six-and-a-half knots, *Mischief* trembling with excitement, the log rotator air-borne, the seas building up and water coming on board, I decided rashly to lower one of the twins. Instead of helping to muzzle the flogging sail Jim, for reasons unknown, smartly let go the halyard of the other sail. The boom dropped in the water and not surprisingly, at the pace we were going, snapped like a carrot. The other boom was sprung, too, but we made it last to Las Palmas. On July 17th we rounded the breakwater and anchored off the Yacht Club.

I see an entry in my diary—'back-ache, cramp, headache, otherwise all right'; an entry which referred to my own infirmities. But it might well have applied to the crew, to Mike certainly, for they went ashore together, spent the night out, and returned with the milk. Mike, by then almost a stretcher case, had had his wallet and other things stolen. Remarkably enough the police recovered them. While staysail booms were being made we painted the deck with red ochre and linseed oil, and the topsides, which at that time were white. Close by lay the twenty-ton ketch *Jenny Wren* bound for Cape Town with a South African crew with whom we naturally fraternized.

The sailing ship route to Cape Town is the same up to a point as for South American ports. After crossing the Equator a vessel stands to the south within 100 or 200 miles of the Brazilian coast. Provided one can carry enough food and water, or replenish with rain water, there is no need to put into a Brazilian port as we did on this voyage. By sailing direct to Cape Town, as we did on the second Crozet voyage, there is a great saving of distance as well as of the time spent in port. Sailing direct we spent seventy-one days at sea and logged 6100 miles. In 1957, when we called at Bahia, or Salvador, the total distance increased by 1500 miles. The fact that we spent only eleven more days at sea was owing to the fast passages we made, averaging ninety-six miles a day from Las Palmas to Bahia, and ninety-two miles a day from Bahia to Cape Town. Normally on a long passage I would not expect much more than seventy miles a day. Perhaps the topmast helped.

We sailed on the evening of July 23rd escorted out by *Jenny Wren*. Hoisting the twins we put her head south-west and went off like a train, logging 770 miles in the first week. As often happens near the Cape Verde Islands, the wind fell light. There were fish about but we could neither hook nor harpoon them. After some assiduous practice at transfixing a tin with the harpoon Jim took his stand at the end of the bowsprit where he remained for hours without any success. Arriving off the island of Sal in the middle of the night we closed what looked like the loom of a light in order to identify it. It was lucky that there were three of us on deck ready to put about, because quite suddenly the loom resolved itself into the lights of a small town, while land, high and menacing, appeared on either side. The next night I spent hours on deck looking for the light on St Jago, the island itself showing as a vague blur on the port bow. No light ever appeared. As someone remarked the Cape Verde islanders ought to have been told that the war was over. In four visits in the vicinity of these islands only once have I seen a light, a light with the pleasing name of Donna Amelia

Albatross in South Atlantic

Shark killed by Lovegrove (with harpoon); Howard Davies and Mike Clay to his right and left on St Vincent. On that occasion the helmsman, a young, sociable chap, must have thought that Donna Amelia herself lived in the lighthouse. Before he saw fit to call me we were practically alongside it, near enough for Donna Amelia, had she been there, to blow kisses.

There is usually so much haze round the islands that one sees nothing and would do better to pass well to the west. But this time we were rewarded with a magnificent and dramatic view of Fogo and its peak of 9281 feet. As the sun rose the clouds slowly lifted like the safety curtain in a theatre revealing bit by bit the steep, violet-coloured slopes of the mountain. Fogo soon disappeared in the haze, for we were sailing fairly fast when Mike chose to go for an involuntary swim. Apparently he fell in while skylarking on the bobstay. I was below trying to sleep when a loud shriek brought me on deck. The lifebuoy had already been thrown over, and after trying in vain to hold on to the log-line Mike let go and swam to the buoy. The correct drill of gybing could not be carried out because we were under the twins which had first to be lowered before we could start motoring back. With a man in the shrouds to keep Mike in sight we handed the twins and within about twenty minutes Mike had been hauled out. I have no record of what was said to the chastened Mike but in any case it would not look well in print. To keep the man in sight is the vital thing and even on this occasion when we acted fairly quickly he was a long way astern and not easy to see.

On a hot, windless day we were all in the sea trying to keep cool when a shark joined the party. Our flailing arms and legs as we rushed for the ship should have frightened it out of its life, but it remained quite calm waiting to be fed. It swallowed a cabbage, a rotten one, with apparent gusto, and nosed broodingly at an empty bully beef tin, but nothing would induce him within the harpooneers reach. The southwest rain-bearing winds which we presently met are known as the south-west Monsoon and are a sort of continuation and deflection of the south-east Trades. They enabled us to fill our tanks, gave us all fresh-water baths, and lasted for a wet, depressing week. At this stage of a voyage to South America only a crew of seagoing philosophers, pranked in reason's garb as well as oilskins, would retain their good humour as the ship bears them steadily away from their destination on the starboard tack. When we had reached as far as Long. 15° W., less than 200 miles from the African coast I became alarmed. Then the wind backed slowly to east of south, we went about, and at last pointed towards Brazil. Pointing towards it though we were, Brazil is a large country with two thousand miles of coastline and we hit it in the wrong place. We made a mess of things. Having crossed the Equator several degrees too far west and plagued by winds that were more south than south-east, we took the easy course and sailed too free. Consequently, helped by the Equatorial current setting us west at the rate of some thirty miles a day, we fetched up three miles off Recife, dimly recognized through a rain storm. Recife is near the extreme north-east corner of South America and over 300 miles north of Bahia. It was humiliating for me, the navigator, to have to go about and stand out to the east. The wise man sits on the hole in his carpet. Recife would have served me as well as Bahia and I could have boldly proclaimed that this had all along been our target. Spending as little time as possible on this unprofitable tack we went about again to steer south, whereupon, the wind heading us, we were soon enjoying a remarkably close and dangerous view of a charming, rustic village, palms, thatched huts, and boats drawn up on the beach. It is not well to make too free with the shore in these parts. From north of Recife down to Bahia the coast is fringed with a barrier reef of coral which lies from a mile to three miles offshore. This reef is about sixteen feet wide at the top, slopes seawards, is abrupt on the land side, and is in general under water.

South of Cape Agostinho the coast trends more west so that we were able to follow it down without having to tack. On August 30th we entered Bahia and anchored off the old port packed tight with local craft. The wide bay that stretches away inland has the lovely, resounding name of Baia de Todos os Santos, the port itself is simply Baia or Bahia, and the city is San Salvador. It is one of the oldest South American cities, founded in 1549. One tends to think that nothing old should exist in the New World, but in San Salvador, or Lima and Santiago, for example, there are great cathedrals and churches dating back three hundred years or more. San Salvador was once the capital of Brazil and the chief port of entry for African slaves; hence the wonderfully mixed population of all colours including full-blooded negroes.

Besides the many richly decorated churches, some built of marble brought from Europe, there are the gloomy stone-built mansions with massive carved doors that were the homes of great merchant princes, their wealth founded mainly on sugar and slaves. The city is in two parts. The old, so-called, built on a narrow strip of land along the water at the foot of a steep, black, 240-foot high cliff. This is the busy commercial quarter surrounding the old port and containing the main market. The upper city is on top of the cliff, and to reach it, besides steps and steep motor roads, there is direct access by means of passenger lifts. After making one lift trip out of curiosity I preferred using the steps, and that these were preferable may be seen from the account of a lift ride in 1880, when E. F. Knight was at Bahia in his boat *Falcon*. In 1957 the aroma of castor oil was not so pronounced but there were many others:

> We take our tickets for the elevator, and enter a half-dark sort of wild-beast cage, where we sit down beside several of the gorgeous fat negresses, for the production of which Bahia is celebrated, and a few dark gentlemen smoking huge Bahia cigars. A strong and not delectable aroma pervades the cage, which seems in some strange way to call up reminiscences of childhood. I have it—it is castor oil. The machinery of the elevator is evidently lubricated with this horror of my youth.

Between us and the shore the old port was choc-a-bloc with strange local craft manned by piratical looking mulattoes and negroes; small fishing boats like spoons, and various big trading craft painted in bold colours, some lateen-rigged with unstayed masts, some fore-and-aft schooners, and some with a loose-footed gaff mainsail and a tall, oblong sail on the foremast. In Knight's book *Cruise of the Falcon* there is a pleasing sketch of one of the latter.

Having taken on provisions, water, and petrol, we sailed for Cape Town on September 9th. *Mischief* then had a petrol engine, the Chrysler 'Crown' engine which had been in her when I bought her in 1954. If given attention it did good service and in Gerry Levick we had the man to give it attention. On the next voyage, partly through neglect and partly through the running down of the starting battery when for two months the engine lay idle, it became a solid mass inside of salt and rust. In addition to supplies we took on two passengers, a pair of budgerigars. They were bought in default of a parrot, for parrots even in their native haunt were outrageously expensive. These two may well have been cock and hen but we called them Peter and Paul; too prophetically, as it turned out, for Peter did fly away. We used to let them fly around in the cabin until one day we forgot to close the skylight and poor Peter vanished. Since we were in mid-ocean there was no hope for him. Paul reached Lymington safely.

CHAPTER XII

CAPE TOWN

———◆———

U NLESS, LIKE THE TRADITIONAL SAILOR, one has a wife in every
port, most ports of the world may be left without regret. It was
good to be at sea, away from the heat, clamour, and smells of Bahia.
Even to a man who is willing to take things as he finds them, it did
not appear to be a salubrious spot—especially the old town, where the
refuse of the market and the quayside provided the luxuries as well
as the necessities of life for a vast colony of rats. The sight of them
at night scurrying across the road and into the covered market was
itself enough to induce symptoms of Bubonic plague. In the words of
the old sweat's song: 'There were rats, rats, big as bloody cats, in the
Quartermaster's store'. Only in the trenches and dug-outs of the First
World War were to be seen such sleek and cheeky rats. Nowadays the
sailor has only the peril of the sea to face, whereas not so many years
ago, if he stayed long at a place like Bahia he stood every chance of
being buried there, a victim to Yellow Jack or typhoid.

From Bahia a sailing vessel has to get further south before it can
steer direct for Cape Town, as far south as Lat. 35°S. when there is a
good prospect of having mainly westerly winds. As well as southing
we made a lot of easting, so that by the time we had run through
the south-east Trades and were in the region of variable winds we
were on the same meridian as when we had crossed the Equator. The
variable winds and variable weather, albatross and whales, were a
refreshing change after the tame sameness of Trade-wind regions and
lifeless tropical seas. Whales do not seem to mistrust small, silent
sailing ships. One evening we had one swimming slowly and majesti-
cally around only some twenty yards from the boat. At night he was
still there, startling the helmsman whenever he came up for a blow.
In common prudence no one dreamt of stirring him up with our
small harpoon but in any case a whale is not the sort of creature one
would wish to harm:

> We do it wrong, being so majestical,
> To offer it the show of violence.

Seen at close range from the deck of a small boat a whale appears so invulnerably vast that one is amazed afresh at the reckless hardihood of the men who used to kill their whales in hand-to-hand fight, as it were—and as they still do at the Azores where they hunt them in sailing and rowing boats. It is one thing to row up to a whale, but the boldest, one imagines, would pause before launching a harpoon at that latent mass of power and fury. It must be like throwing a match into a powder magazine.

The albatross were just as interested in us as we were in them. Having watched us go by they would take off again in their clumsy way, flapping their great wings and pedalling hard with their feet, fly ahead of us and alight in order to have yet another good look at *Mischief*. If we were becalmed a small flock of them would gather round, more out of curiosity than in expectation of food. We tried floating potatoes out to them on a bit of board but they were not amused. When a shark appeared, we were surprised that it took no notice of these sitting albatross, for it would have had no difficulty in hoisting in one or two to make a juicy and satisfying meal. Perhaps feathers are too indigestible even for a shark. Anyhow this unfortunate shark paid for its indifference as to what was going on. Jim harpooned it and after a brief struggle we got him on board. He was only about six feet long and his small teeth did not look very formidable. We ate it, and except that there were no bones it was quite the nastiest fish that I have ever eaten, tasting like warm, slightly greasy, blancmange, and eminently sick-making. Jim, who had a vested interest in it, professed to enjoy it and astonished us by eating the liver for breakfast.

On October 11th we crossed the Greenwich meridian, thus marking another milestone on our long passage. For the next eight months we were to remain in the eastern hemisphere. The weather, like the British economy, continued to be of the 'stop-go' variety. On one of the 'stop' days we recorded an all-time low of ten miles, followed hard by *Mischief*'s best ever, a run of 151 miles in twenty-four hours. At Jim's instigation we had unlaced the mainsail from the boom and ran with it loose-footed. Thus the sail had a lot more belly, and although the risks of a 'Chinese' gybe were not obviated, the consequences would have been less damaging—provided, of course, that the helmsman avoided being strangled or beheaded by the main-sheet. The great drawback was that the sail had to be lowered for reefing.

The sighting of ships, seals basking on the surface, and the mooing of penguins at night, assured us that land was not far off. Some thought these penguin noises were like cows mooing, while others likened the noise to that made by the old-fashioned motor horn that one squeezed. They were Jackass penguins which breed on a few of the islands off the west coast of South Africa. They are valued and protected on account of the guano and eggs they produce; few people are permitted to visit the islands. The eggs are in so great demand at Cape Town and Johannesburg that they have to be ordered in advance. It was a supremely satisfying moment when we sighted land early on the morning of October 3rd. To cross an ocean and make a landfall on another continent gives the amateur sailor similar satisfaction to the climbing of a peak. By evening, when Table Mountain and Lion's Head were easily recognisable, we were still twenty miles away. The lights of Robben Island and Green Point came up and at midnight we sailed slowly through the wide entrance to Duncan Dock. We had hoped to anchor there till morning but a police launch drew alongside and brusquely ordered us to anchor outside. In spite of our two South Africans who spoke the same language they regarded us with suspicion. Next morning they made amends by bringing off a pilot who took us into the small, crowded yacht basin, the home of the Royal Cape Yacht Club. We had been forty-four days at sea.

We stayed a month at Cape Town, a week longer than I had anticipated owing to the defection of Pat Green and some delay in finding a replacement. For the whole period my diary is a complete blank and for the two interesting facets of Cape Town, the mountain and the sea, I have drawn largely from the account of the second visit. There can be no more congenial a place, or one with more facilities for the cruising yachtsman to refresh and refit, than Cape Town, in particular at the Royal Cape Yacht Club. Help and hospitality are offered in embarrassing profusion. The members are ready with not only advice but with practical help, and since among them there are men of almost every trade, profession, or business there are few problems that one or other of them cannot tackle.

Among these keen, experienced sailors, there are many who have built or are capable of building their own boats. Perhaps the absence of yards devoted to building or repairing yachts is even more pronounced in South Africa than in Australia, so that practical knowledge and ability in that line is more common than it is at home.

Although conditions there are not altogether favourable, a goodly number of ocean-going yachts, day sailers, and dinghies are maintained afloat. Table Bay is a fine stretch of water, but along the coast to the east or to the west small harbours and anchorages are scarce. And in order to reach, say, Port Elizabeth, East London, or Durban, one must pass the notoriously stormy Cape and contend with the fast-flowing Agulhas current. Merely maintaining a boat in the yacht basin has some discouraging aspects. In summer southeasters are frequent and violent, sweeping across the unsheltered basin, carrying with them so much sand and gravel that a boat's varnish and paintwork is most efficiently sandblasted. Alternatively, when the wind is north-west it blows smoke from the docks to blacken the rigging. And if that is not enough there are numbers of sea-birds that love to roost on the boats in the yacht basin, in defiance of their being festooned with bird-scarers in the shape of fluttering rags, nets, and such like, so that a boat's deck soon becomes a miniature guano island. Worst of all, perhaps, is the effect on wooden decks and hulls of the hot sun of long, rainless summers.

Having in the closest proximity a magnificent mountain there is naturally a flourishing Mountain Club at Cape Town, a club that is unique in having its principal playground only a mile or two from its headquarters. In the eyes of a mountaineer Table Mountain would be more pleasing if it culminated in a peak instead of being crowned with a flat plateau. The cragsman, with eyes only for its precipitous face, will want nothing added. Whatever the average citizens of Cape Town may feel about their mountain, to the climber, as his eye wanders over the great wall towering aloof from the busy city, the dark gullies, the gaunt precipices and the steep buttresses, are a daily inspiration and challenge. Like all mountains it has its moods, one day smiling in sun-bathed serenity, the next frowning grimly under a blanket of cloud from which ragged streamers rush down the gullies.

On the miles of more or less continuously steep face of the mountain there are hundreds of climbing routes, from easy to those 'beyond the bounds of human possibility', on ridge, buttress, face, or gully, and of varying degrees of length and exposure. On occasions a few friends in the Mountain Club would forgo their own fun for the sake of taking me up one of the easier climbs. Mike Clay, of course, went off with younger friends in search of sterner stuff. The week-end climbing had a far from solemn ritual of its own. Not very early on a Sunday morning cars disgorge parties of men and women in shorts, bare-legged and bare-armed, at the foot of the track. Though the day was already hot the shorts made me shudder. In rock-climbing the use of the knees is frowned upon, though I myself have always found them useful; but I was not thinking of that so much as the fact that upon all the paths to the climbs and upon the plateau, there is an assorted variety of vegetation, some of it extremely virulent. As well as thorns and razor-edged cacti, there is the blister-bush, only needing to be touched to raise a crop of blisters. The rich and varied flora is by no means all noxious—flowering heaths, brooms, proteas in profusion, lilies, gladioli, and ground orchids of all colours including the justly famed Red Disa. These flowers, which alone make a mountain walk worth while, are wisely protected, all collecting being forbidden.

From the climber's point of view this profuse vegetation might be deemed superfluous but it is not really so. On the steep faces where most of the serious climbing is done the rock is fairly clean. On the buttresses and in the gullies, though the plants and trees might offend the purist, they come in handy for belays, handholds, and above all fuel. For the Sunday parties that we left assembling are expedition-minded, fully aware that climbers as well as armies march on their stomachs. After an hour's stroll along the well graded track, the arid, stony slopes of the mountain on the one hand, and on the other, far below, the boundless ocean, we come to a convenient spring and abundant firewood. Out of capacious rucksacks come the smoke-grimed billies, veterans of countless bivouacs and *al fresco* meals, to be balanced cunningly on stones or on the traditional forked sticks over swiftly kindled fires. Of what use are spirit lamps and similar 'cissy' contrivances when there is meat to be broiled or charred? After our modest 'elevenses', tea, chops, and a couple of eggs, the fires are carefully quenched and the various parties peel off on lesser tracks leading to the foot of their chosen climb. By now it is sizzling hot and shorts seem the only wear despite blister bushes and thorns. If the heat threatens to be excessive, our leader may pick on a climb with a view to remaining in the shade, a refinement that the traditionally hardy mountaineer would seem to adopt by accident rather than design.

In any case our climb is a deliberate affair, fitting in the circumstances; a hot day, a party of five or more, and the presence of an elderly mariner straight from sea, besides all the hauling up of sacks with their precious contents. Shady or sunny, the climb will certainly have been chosen with a proper regard for luncheon sites, that is to say the necessity for finding wood and water at or near the top of the climb. In high summer when some of the springs and water pockets may be dry, someone in the party skilled in bush-craft, a descendant possibly of the 'voortrekkers,' will know where water may be found. The equipment of a well-found party such as ours will certainly include a length of plastic tubing for siphoning water out of inaccessible crannies. Water having been found, the party scatters to collect firewood, and in no time the billies are boiling and the steaks broiling on long wooden skewers. This is the highlight of the day. Perched on our mountain eyrie, replete with food and drink, we can gaze out upon the deep indigo sea where fishing boats crawl like water beetles and the rollers break lazily on dazzling white beaches. The descent is usually by one of the many gullies, preferably on the shady side of the mountain, and having at its foot a convenient spring where we can brew up for the third and last time.

The younger climbers and the Tigers, of whom there are plenty in the Club, might scorn such a picnic. There are those, however, who love the mountains for their own sake, for whom it is enough to be on a mountain either alone or with good companions; many like myself whose years may have calmed their climbing passions without dulling their faculty for enjoying the sort of day I have described. I suspect that on this occasion the wind may have been tempered, that out of regard for one who had not yet got his land-legs the arrangements for the party's well-being were slightly more elaborate than usual.

Besides Table Mountain there are in Cape Province alone mountains and mountain ranges from 5000 feet to 9000 feet high, not well known and little climbed, which offer plenty of strenuous climbing and the pioneering of new routes. The only drawback to South African mountaineering, and I see no way of remedying it, is that there are no glaciers. By its proximity Table Mountain is the main scene of activity, and the Club is its vigilant guardian against those who would like to push the suburbs of Cape Town ever higher up its slopes or to build a motor road to the summit. The Club, too, is organised to take care of the fairly frequent accidents to pedestrians and visitors. Tourists disgorged on the summit by the cable-way get lost and have to be brought down; or sometimes, owing to a sudden storm, the cable-car is unable to descend, and the whole car-load of tourists stranded on top have to be shepherded down. To a newcomer the cable-way is inevitably something of an eyesore, especially the terminus building perched on the edge of a fine crag.

The Yacht Club has its own slipway with a winch powerful enough to haul up a boat of *Mischief*'s displacement, about thirty-five tons. We had no drawings from which the experts could see the under-water shape of her lines, but they made a good guess, adjusted the cradle accordingly, and hauled her up without mishap. After a good scrub down we put on a fresh coat of anti-fouling paint, using the contents of a five-gallon drum that had been given me at Valparaiso by a generous shipowner. We might as well have applied face powder. By the time we were on the way home we could see patches of bare wood below the water-line. At Lymington, when the boat had been hauled out, we found that many of the planks, mostly forward of the beam, were riddled with teredo worm. Sections of the planks were like honey-comb, and for part of the homeward run we cannot have had as much as half an inch of sound wood between us and the sea. Some two hundred running feet of planking had to be renewed.

Pat Green, as I have noted, did not keep his word and volunteers to take his place were by no means as plentiful as blackberries. In fact we had but one, young Allen Jolly aged eighteen, who after dithering for some time finally made up his mind to come. It surprised me that the hard-bitten sailing men of the Club did not consider our prospects were very bright. In their opinion, if we were still afloat, we might fetch up in Australia, certainly not at the Crozet, and shook their heads mournfully at so rash an enterprise. It is always gratifying to confound the experts, so that when their dismal forebodings were in part fulfilled, the pill was the more bitter.

CHAPTER XIII

DEFEATED

WITH STORES AND WATER ONBOARD, and *Mischief* having been stripped for the fight by the sending down of her topmast, we made ready to sail. On the afternoon of November 21st we weaved our way out of the yacht basin and hoisted sail in the spacious Duncan Dock. In spite of the size of the dock the wind played some odd tricks. I noticed that as we passed about a hundred yards from a vessel moored alongside, her ensign and ours were streaming out in exactly opposite directions. After twice going about in a reasonably seaman-like manner we cleared the entrance where a crowd of wellwishers and photographers had assembled. That was almost as far as we went that day, and two days later we were still drifting on a glassy sea a few miles from the Green Point lighthouse. At last, drifting and sailing, we had enough wind to take our departure from Cape Point thirty miles south of Table Bay. Cape Point at the extremity of the Cape of Good Hope is not quite the southernmost tip of the continent. Cape Aghulas, eighty miles farther east, is some thirty miles farther south.

Out of regard for the tales of woe told us by the Club Cassandras we treated the waters south of the Cape with respect. From the start we had two men on watch in four-hour watches. It meant a short sleep, for if one had the first watch from 8 p.m. to midnight, one came on again at 4 a.m. Formerly we had been doing single watches of three hours. Young Jolly was at first off colour, unable to enjoy the tunny we caught and which Howard served up poached in white wine and herbs. But it was not long before we had other things to think about than fishing. On the 26th, when we were about 500 miles on our way, in Lat. 39° S., the wind hardened to a moderate gale; a heavy swell from north-west, rain, and a steadily falling glass, promised worse to come. We had already reefed down but by nightfall we changed to storm canvas, try-sail and storm jib. Next day as we sped south-east before rising wind and sea we tried to slow her down by handing both sails and streaming

163

a heavy warp. It made little difference, under bare poles she still ran at four knots thanks to the windage offered by the heavy shrouds and rigging. Two more warps were streamed in big bights but on the 28th we still logged 100 miles. It was certainly blowing.

Without any sails to help, steering became tricky and if a big sea kicked her stern round, prompt, vigorous action was needed to correct the slew. No storms last for ever and I began to think after two days that this one had lasted quite long enough; for the sea was building up and waves beginning to topple over and break with ominous frequency. That evening the glass steadied at 28.6, the wind backed a couple of points, the sky momentarily cleared, and for a brief moment sunlight glistened upon the streaming, lurching deck of old *Mischief*, the lonely centrepiece of a wild, desolate scene. As night closed in fierce and increasingly heavy squalls of wind and rain, accompanied by thunder and lightning, began sweeping across the sky, the prelude to a foul night. Although the glass showed signs of a rise, when I went below at 8 p.m. I could not offer the crew much comfort:

> I tell you naught for your comfort,
> Yea, naught for your desire,
> Save that the sky grows darker yet
> And the seas rise higher.

Two days of gale conditions damp the spirits and impair the efficiency of most crews; the incessant whine of the wind, the hiss and surge of great seas breaking alongside, at length begin to daunt even the least apprehensive. The general uproar, the ship's motion, and the strain of waiting for something to happen, make sleep hard to come by. Knowing that it is useless I never even try, but just lie with ears cocked waiting for a new note in the wind or some unwonted noise that might spell calamity. Of the two men on watch one sat lashed in the cockpit steering, the other stood by on the companion-way steps looking out astern over the top of the weather boards that in rough weather are fitted to keep water out of the combined chart and engine-room. As the waves increased in height the helmsman's job became more difficult, trying to keep her stern on to the seas either by steering the given course or by watching the run of the waves. In daylight the latter method is at times frightening and on a dark night impossible. Waves do not all run true and with a heavy boat like *Mischief*, slow on the helm, the smartest helmsman cannot act quickly enough to dodge or square her up before a dangerously breaking sea. When she yawed wildly the helmsman had to sweat to get her back on course before she broached to, a position in which, without sails, she would no longer steer.

At this time we had a canvas weather dodger mounted on heavy iron stanchions practically surrounding the cockpit. It was a nuisance in that it hindered a man from moving quickly from the cockpit to the deck; and I had a feeling that it tempted the helmsman to keep his head down in shelter thus preventing him from keeping a good look-out all round. In this storm the dodger got swept away and I have not yet fitted another, contrary to the present day tendency to shut the crew in behind dodgers, hoods like motor cars, and Perspex glass screens. No doubt these keep the helmsman dry but they must impair the efficiency of the look-out. In crews I have had, some are apt to think that the helmsman's job ends with steering, forgetting that he has also to keep a faithful look-out, noting everything in sight, ships, birds, clouds, the wind, the waves, and much else. In fair weather some go on watch with a book under their arm so that as soon as the skipper is away below they can lash the tiller and enjoy a quiet read.

Coming on watch again at midnight I thought the weather had worsened, the wind backing west and blowing harder as the barometer rose. Hardly any two people will agree in their estimate of wind force, and probably no two people when it comes to estimating the height of waves. I thought this wind had been blowing at force 9 for most of the time, more in gusts. I had not been long in the cockpit, too busy with the tiller to ponder much over the vicissitudes of life at sea, when a wave broke over the counter, ripped away most of the dodger, broke off two of its stanchions, and half-filled the capacious cockpit with water. The cockpit drains itself by means of two pipes leading outboard, but the pipes are small, and long before much draining has been done most of the water finds its way below by way of the lockers under the cockpit seats. No harm in that, because it all collects in the well of the bilge whence it can be pumped out. What with rain, spray, and the working of the boat there was always some water below which we cleared by a few minutes pumping every half-hour using the rotary pump mounted in the heads.

Moroni, Grand Comore Island

Gerry and I rerigged the dodger after a fashion, more as a gesture of defiance than for the protection it gave. How illusory this protection was Mike Clay presently learnt. Soon after six, daylight, and Mike at the helm, a sea struck the port side just forward of the quarter. It seemed that Mike had bent down under the cockpit seat trying to light a cigarette, a difficult feat in the driving spray and a dangerous one, for we had nearly broached to. The sea demolished the remains of the dodger, flattened all its stanchions, and started inboard the cockpit coaming which in turn wrenched up the adjacent deck plank. Water spurted through every seam of the skylight while the fenders and two heavy blocks lashed abaft the skylight went for six. The spare spars lashed on deck came adrift but luckily remained on board. On its way forward the wave swept the dinghy overboard, bending at right angles the life-line stanchions as it went. With the dinghy we lost a bag of anthracite, two small water tanks, the working jib folded and lashed, and several coils of rope. So much for the deck; except, of course, for the unlucky Mike who had been thrown violently to the cockpit floor, half drowned and half dazed.

At the time I was below where the immediate results of the blow were chaotic. She leaned right over, a cataract came down the companion way and through the skylight, and everything moveable alighted on the floor to swim about in the water. In the engine room all the bosun's stores and tools had leapt off the shelves to finish up in the bilge or less accessible crannies. While the other man on watch struggled to get her back on course, the rest began clearing up the mess below, salvaging sodden books and clothing, and pumping out the water swilling about over the cabin sole. Jim and I then went forward to set the storm jib to help in keeping her before the wind. Meantime the weather had begun to improve in so much as the sun shone brilliantly, though wind and sea showed little sign of abating. A veil of spray blown off the wave tops covered the surface of the sea which now became more confused as the wind backed to south-west. Frequently two monster waves would collide and tower up into a fearsome pyramid of water.

By next day the wind had gone down. We took in the warps, streamed the log and set more sail. As the wind moderated the waves that had long been subjected to its tyranny expressed their new found freedom by leaping higher and running all ways. One such now sprang on board and completed the ruin on deck by breaking up the deck locker abaft the mast. The time had come for us to take stock of the damage and decide what to do. The damage was superficial and easily repairable but the loss of the dinghy was fatal to our plan of landing on the Crozet Islands. An American climbing friend, when he heard what had happened, disagreed on this: 'What worries me about your last trip,' he wrote, 'is that the Tilman I knew would have swum ashore rather than admit defeat.' Well, may be not. Even twenty years before, the time when he and I had been climbing together, I should have had more sense than to try swimming ashore at the Crozet.

No, the only reasonable alternative was to go to Kerguelen where we should be able to land at the French base. But Kerguelen was still the best part of 2000 miles away in Lat. 49° S. and we were only on the edge of the Forties. 'If they do these things in the green tree, what shall be done in the dry?' I wondered weakly how many more such batterings we would receive in the course of those 2000 miles, whereas a man of more robust mind would have argued that the weather had done its worst, that we had come through in tolerably good shape, and that since the summer was advancing we were unlikely to meet with any more such breezes lasting for three days. Another worrying thought was that besides myself only two of the crew could be relied upon to steer safely in bad weather, and the prospect of that long haul under those conditions so daunted me that prudence decided me to give up and sail back to Durban. 'Prudence', as the Sage says, 'quenches that ardour of enterprise by which everything is done that can claim praise or admiration, and represses that generous temerity which often fails and often succeeds.' Had we not succeeded at the second attempt two years later this feeble decision would have been another cause for life-long regret, one more to be added to a fairly long list of might-have-beens. On balance I think we did right to give up since we no longer had any chance of achieving what we had set out to do.

So in fine bright weather, a long uneasy swell still running, we put *Mischief*'s head north-east. Though naturally oppressed by our acknowledged failure, none of the crew demurred and none were in favour of trying to reach Kerguelen. We were much nearer to Durban than Cape Town and by going there we should not be obliged to listen to the inevitable refrain, 'We told you so.' Ten days of light winds brought us to a point sixty miles south of Durban, on the edge of the Agulhas current. From the Mozambique Channel southwards the Agulhas current extends from thirty to a hundred miles off the coast and runs at nearly two knots, sometimes much more. The greatest strength recorded is 120 miles a day in the month of September. Close inshore there is a counter-current setting up the coast. Steamers bound east from Cape Town hug the coast so closely that when seen from the offing they appear to be navigating with the utmost recklessness. Helped by a fine north-east breeze we made across the current and got well in under the land. Our proximity to the shore, a black night, and an appalling thunderstorm, combined to give us some anxious hours. In the early hours of the morning the peak halyard parted, but we were about to lower the mainsail anyway on account of the wind, the opening blast of an approaching gale that sent us scurrying along until by morning we were outside Durban. A pilot boarded us and laid us alongside the fish wharf against which we were unmercifully pounded by the wind, now at gale force. Seeing our plight, the Vice-Commodore of the Yacht Club directed us to a sheltered spot where at half-ebb we bumped on the bottom. We then sought to make fast at the end of the steamer wharf but were chased away, and finally we found a home in the yacht basin moored at the uttermost end of a long trot. In the princely way they do things in South Africa the Yacht club ran an all-round-the-clock launch service for taking crews ashore. To signal for the launch the yacht hoisted a 'G' flag. That was the theory, but before we had provided ourselves with another dinghy we had some very long waits. I managed to buy a second-hand eight-foot dinghy made of teak.

Howard Davies left us here. He had played his part manfully, and in fair weather or foul stuck cheerfully to his uninviting task. Throughout the recent gale, when cooking in our galley might have baffled a seagoing conjuror, he had served meals bang on time and in between kept the watch on deck happy with frequent mugs of coffee or cocoa. Alan Jolly returned prematurely to his anxious parents in Cape Town, and with him went Mike Clay. To use an out-dated expression, courting rather than climbing had occupied much of Mike's time in Cape Town, and now he was all on fire to clinch matters by getting married. It was not for me to stand in his way; I could only pronounce a seamanlike blessing and express the hope that married life would run smoother than his brief life at sea. We had thus three berths to fill and for a voyage to England through tropic seas there were enough volunteers. David Smith, a tall lad of eighteen, whose ambition was to be a London 'bobby', took over the galley. Douglas Moor and Ian Sibbald, both inexperienced, came as hands.

In order to salve something from the wreck of our hopes we wanted to return home by way of the Indian Ocean where there were one or two islands of interest that we might visit. Some stores for the homeward voyage, which originally would have been through the Atlantic, had been left at Cape Town, and I now had them sent on to Beira for us to collect. Our friends at the Durban Yacht Club were almost as discouraging as those at Cape Town had been. They were not prophets of doom but they went so far as to say that the passage to Beira in a yacht was not possible. The few yachts that had left Durban for Beira had all had to return, baffled by light winds and the Aghulas current.

Feeling no temptation to spend Christmas in Durban, which at this time of year is exceedingly hot and muggy, I intended sailing on December 22nd. As the Arabs say, the camel-driver has his thoughts and the camel, he has his. The crew, who had been ashore all night did not turn up until late afternoon, evidently not in a seagoing mood; and since it was raining and blowing hard we probably did well not to sail. When we left on the 23rd we started to tack up the coast close inshore hoping to gain some northing before launching out across the current. By evening all the new hands were seasick, so rather than spend a sleepless night working the ship short-handed, we stood out to sea. A force 6 wind at north-east sent us along at six knots and although we lost a lot of ground to the south, by Christmas Day we were out of the current and able to steer north. The crew, too, had recovered sufficiently to face our Christmas dinner of cold ham, Christmas pudding with rum butter, port and cigars.

We made a fast and trouble-free passage to Beira, utterly confounding the Durban prophets of woe. Keeping 200 miles off the coast until well inside the Mozambique channel, we luckily picked up a fresh north-easterly breeze just when we were ready to make our run in across the current. On that day of the passage we logged 150 miles. The chart for the approaches to Beira is a discouraging document, the absence of water and the presence of shoals makes it look more like a map. For fifteen miles out from the port there are acres and acres of sandbanks, or rather mudbanks, deposited by the Pungwe River, a twin brother of the 'grey-green, greasy Limpopo'. Through the banks runs a tenuous, buoyed channel, a channel that at low water ceases to be continuous. Like politics, navigation is the art of the possible, that is to say that sometimes one must be content with an approximation to the intended aim. At dawn of January 3rd, 1958, when we were off the mouth of the Pungwe hoping to see one at least of the many buoys, even if not the precise one aimed at, nothing could be seen at all—no buoys, no ships, no land. Staring without inspiration at the monotonous brown sweep of the horizon at last we made out a ship apparently at anchor. On closing it we found the *Tintagel Castle* anchored near 'P' buoy, the pilot station, and nearby the pilot cutter. When the flood started to run, a pilot came on board. We would have liked to impress this Portuguese mariner with our smooth efficiency. But the engine refused to start, under a strong wind and tide the cable was bar taut, and we had a rare struggle getting the anchor. The mainsail went up in a fashion that suggested we were hoisting it for the first time, and the couple of crashing gybes that we presently executed must have made the Portuguee think that some of us would not live long enough to hoist it again. We made No. 3 buoy without having to gybe, and with the wind on the beam and a three-knot tide under us we rushed from buoy to buoy as if bent on overhauling the *Tintagel Castle*. The pilot anchored us in two-and-a-half fathoms less than a cable from the wharf, in what we were assured was excellent holding ground. It needed to be. The flow of the ebb tide at springs with the river behind it made one dizzy to watch.

Beira, the original Sofala, was visited by Vasco da Gama in 1502 and a few years later the Portuguese established a settlement. San Salvador had been settled at much the same time, both places are in roughly the same latitude, well within the tropics, yet no two places could be more unlike. At Beira there are no sixteenth-century churches and no mansions fitting for merchant princes; none of the busy, teeming life of the waterfront and no picturesque sailing craft; no vast covered market, not even any fresh vegetables, potatoes, or eggs. It is modern, neat, orderly, fairly clean and remarkably dull. On account of the strong tides and the cluster of boats round the one landing place it was not easy to get ashore; and having got there a walk through the town proved to be, in the words of Baedeker, fatiguing and not repaying.

For watering we had to have three 40-gallon drums brought alongside, and having done that and got our provisions from Cape Town on board we were ready to go. As usual the crew made their last night a late night, only David and I stayed on board for supper. It was the height of springs*, two days after the full moon, with the ebb, which runs for seven to eight hours, going like a mill-race. Sitting quietly below after supper in a state of semi-somnolence we were presently aroused by noises off. It seemed a bit early for the crew to have returned. Going on deck I was surprised to find two launches alongside. The town of Beira, the wharf, and the ship that had been lying just ahead of us, seemed in some mysterious way to have receded almost out of sight, and were in fact still fast receding. We were adrift, nearly two miles on the way out to sea. A steamer anchored nearby and several others lying downstream, must have all just missed being run down. Apparently *Mischief*'s departure outward bound, stern first, like a ghost ship with nobody on deck, had been noticed by some alert chap in the port office. While we were being towed back—and against the sluicing tide the launch had its work cut out—David and I got up the anchor. The motor car tyre that now adorned one of its flukes must have been hooked 'en passant', as chess players say.

---

*   Spring tides, the highest-ranging in the lunar cycle—Ed.

CHAPTER XIV

COMORO AND ALDABRA ISLANDS

A S THE COMORO ISLANDS lie athwart the northern exit from the
Mozambique Channel we decided to visit Île Grande Comore,
the biggest of the group of four. This island is the seat of the French
Resident and it also has on it a Mont Kartala, 7874 feet high. Mont
Kartala is a volcano, having last erupted in 1918, and it was therefore
unlikely to be of much interest. The majority of volcanoes have placid,
cindery slopes—Teneriffe is a steep exception—rather to be avoided
than climbed.

Sailing early on January 8th we made our way from buoy to buoy
down the channel, taking our departure from the outermost. Again
we started by hugging the African coast where hot, clammy weather,
light winds and little progress, soon frayed our tempers. Taking
advantage of a fine northerly breeze we stood over to the Madagascar
side of the channel, losing some ground to the south on the way and
not finding much better winds. We had already been out a fortnight
when we sighted the casuarina trees and buildings on Juan de Nova,
a small guano island sixty miles off the Madagascar coast. Another
hundred miles to the north-west is Chesterfield Islet and I must have
thought myself on a par with Henry the Navigator to expect to sight
that, for the islet is a mere ten-foot-high rock fringed by a sand-cov-
ered reef. According to my reckoning we had already passed it when
Gerry, climbing the shrouds to retrieve a pair of shorts hung up to
dry, spotted the rock fine on the bow. As we passed it a few cables off
we noticed that the reef was covered with frigate birds. We did well
to get away from the small islands and islets that lie far out from this
part of the Madagascar coast, and not to try to spot any more. During
the next four days we experienced some remarkably bad weather, an
unbroken pall of low cloud, prolonged squalls of wind and rain, and
a rough sea. To account for such an unusual spell I suspected there
might be a tropical storm in the vicinity and felt accordingly anxious.

January is the worst month of the cyclone season in this part of the Indian Ocean. While it is rare for these storms to cross the high land of Madagascar, a few occasionally pass north of the island and recurve to enter the Mozambique Channel.

When the weather at last cleared we made out Anjouan, one of the Comoro Islands, some forty miles away, and three days later we fetched Moroni on the west side of Grand Comoro. It is the only harbour and a bad one, encumbered with coral reefs and wide open except to the east. Lying at the small stone pier a boat spends much of the time bumping on the bottom and when afloat it is bashed against the wall by the swell. The anchorage is on the seaward slope of the reef where with offshore winds the anchor may drag into deep water, while with onshore winds the stern hits the reef. The inner harbour, used by dhows, dries out. The six-thousand-odd inhabitants live clustered round the inner harbour and the mosque in a rabbit-warren of flat-roofed houses built of coral rag. Beyond, slightly aloof, are the Residency, a bank, and the Grand Hotel, fighting a losing battle against dilapidation and an absence of guests. The people are a mixture of Arab, Persian, Malagasy, and African negroes, speaking various dialects with Swahili and pigeon-French for common use. There are a few French settlers engaged in growing vanilla and ylang-ylang, a shrub of grotesque growth having pleasantly scented flowers from which an essential oil is extracted. Grand Comoro is the least fertile island of the group, parts of it being mere lava desert, and in spite of a copious rainfall there are neither rivers nor wells. As might be expected the inhabitants are of a conservative nature, either too proud, too poor, or too wise, to delight much in progress. I saw only two jeeps and not a boat in the harbour that boasted an engine. While we were there a Messageries passenger ship arrived with hundreds of deck passengers who, with their baggage, had all to be landed in rowing boats or even in dug-outs propelled by paddles. Admittedly one or two of the rowing boats were more like State barges rowed by twelve pairs of oars.

As we passed through the rabbit-warren in search of the Residency the white-robed Arabs lounging round the mosque either scowled at the infidels or religiously averted their gaze. But the Resident welcomed us kindly and waived all formalities. Having had a drink at the dreary hotel we had about exhausted Moroni's attractions, but Gerry made friends with some of the French with whom he made a successful assault on Kartala. We had long had this great bulge in view during our deliberate approach to the island and it had every appearance of offering another of Baedeker's fatiguing and not repaying excursions. Nor was I willing to leave the boat for the couple of days that would be required in view of the hazards of the harbour, the likelihood of theft, and the habit the crew had of absenting themselves when needed. The possession of one's own boat certainly enables one to visit many outlandish places, yet in some cases the need to look after the boat may prevent one seeing much of them.

I was not sorry to get away on the evening of February 4th, the more so because we had just suffered a long spell of pier-bashing awaiting the belated arrival of two of the crew. Our immediate destination was the small coral atoll of Aldabra about 220 miles to the north-east. None of us had seen a coral atoll and my interest had been aroused by reading about Aldabra in *The Cruise of the Cachalot*, the stirring story of an old-time whaling ship by Frank Bullen. Whaling captains of the old school were strongly averse to calling anywhere, both to avoid port dues and desertion on the part of the crew. After cruising round the Comoro Islands and collecting 800 barrels of sperm-whale oil, the skipper of the *Cachalot*, in need of water, put into a cove, rather than any of the ports.

> No whaling captain [says Bullen] would be so reckless as to incur port charges; the islands offer great inducements to whaling captains to call, since no one but men hopelessly mad would venture to desert in such places. That qualification is the chief one for any place to possess in the eyes of a whaling captain.

After watering, the *Cachalot* had proceeded to Aldabra, where desertion was even less likely, in order to give the men a run on shore and to collect seabirds eggs and green turtles.

We were a good deal slower than even the lumbering old *Cachalot*. Four days elapsed before we had sunk the great bulk of Kartala and another five before we sighted Aldabra. Across this stretch of the Indian Ocean the Equatorial current sets briskly to the west, the atoll is but a few miles wide and only some fifty feet high, so that here was a case when the navigator experienced the breeze of anxiety playing freshly upon the brow of expectation. An island landfall, preferably at dawn, has a sharp, ecstatic flavour of its own. At first a pale green shimmer in the sky ahead, the reflected light from the shallow water of the lagoon, hinted at what lay beneath, and presently the dark green of its few trees broke the sharp, blue horizon. As we approached the settlement at the northwest corner of the atoll the manager came off in a pirogue rowed by six muscular, cheerful negroes. Visitors are rare, and the schooner from the Seychelles on its bi-annual trip was not due for a month, so they were pleased to see us and to exchange small gifts—cigarettes and bully beef on our side, eggs, coconuts, and limes, on theirs.

There are actually four islands, West, Polymnie, Main, and South, divided by narrow passes, the whole forming an atoll enclosing a lagoon. They are a dependency of the Seychelles and leased to the Seychelles Company. The *Pilot* thus describes Aldabra:

> The atoll is either coral or coral rock. The seaward face has abrupt overhanging cliffs from 12 to 15 feet high; the surface of the islands is from 12 to 20 feet high and the sand dunes reach an elevation of from 50 to 60 feet. The islands are clothed in places by a thick almost impenetrable jungle of pemphis, the plants being from 12 to 15 feet high, and mangrove forests flourish, some of the clumps being from 70 to 80 feet in height. The fringing reef is everywhere narrow, never extending more than 3 cables offshore. The chief industries are the preparation and export of dried fish, calipee, dried turtle meat, fish oils, and a little copra. The giant land tortoise is to be found in some numbers on Main Island, and less commonly through the rest of the atoll. Green turtles are to be found, of which there are two distinct groups; one resident, the other migratory and visiting the atoll in vast hordes from December to April to breed. In 1923 wild goats were plentiful. Rats are a great plague and the islands are also infested with jiggers.

The population, or perhaps crew, of the island comprises some seventy souls, men, women, and children, natives of the Seychelles and employees of the company which leases the island to exploit the fishing and the turtle. Every two years the crew is relieved and twice a year a schooner brings stores—mainly rice for the fishermen and their families, and salt for curing—and takes away dried fish, turtle meat, calipee, and turtle shell. A minor source of income is the giant land tortoise, akin to those found on the Galapagos, a few of which are supplied to various zoos. On the beach we saw a pen containing about thirty of these creatures dozing in the sun, awaiting shipment.

The turtle are harpooned in the sea or turned over and subsequently killed when they come up the beach to lay. A turtle lays up to 200 eggs in a hole in the sand dug with its fore-flippers well above tide mark, and goes back to sea on the next tide. After forty days the eggs hatch out almost simultaneously but only a few of the baby turtles survive. On the short trek down to the beach to the sea for which they instinctively make, many are killed by the rapacious frigate birds, while those that reach the sea are preyed upon by sharks and other fish. Only some ten per cent reach maturity. Down wind of the manager's house were the racks where the turtle meat and calipee were drying. Calipee (beloved of Jos Sedley) is well enough in turtle soup but smells vilely when being dried. It is a product of the green turtle, so called from the colour of the fat, and is the tissue joining the flesh to the shell. Only about 3 lb of calipee is got from a turtle, their average weight being 300 lb.

Piloted by the manager, we motored round the north-west corner of the atoll to enter Main Channel, the deepest pass into the lagoon, where we anchored. At springs the tide runs through the pass at the rate of six knots with scarcely any slack water. Some of the crew went off in the dinghy to explore West Island, but exploring on Aldabra is a formidable, time-consuming task. The surface of metamorphosed coral rock—it rings like metal when walked upon—is jagged and pitted with large and small cavities. Much of it is covered with a stubborn jungle of pemphis wood, the living trees and the dead trunks so hopelessly intertwined that without a cutting party it is well-nigh impenetrable. We only fully realized the strength of the tide when the dinghy party's first attempt to return ended in failure. They had to seize their brief chance at slack water. In the evening I went ashore alone with a sleeping bag and some food to spend the night on Polymnie Island on the east side of the pass. Besides other reasons it was my birthday so I gave myself a present of a romantic but far from comfortable night. It was the only night I had ashore in the course of this thirteen-months' voyage.

Pirates used not to restrict their activities to the Spanish Main. The Indian Ocean offered a wide and rich field for these enterprising mariners, and its many islands secure places for their refreshment—particularly a place like Aldabra with its turtle and giant tortoise, for the latter's ability to live without food for many days provides a ship's company with an ideally economic supply of meat on the hoof. It is fitting then that this lonely, tropical island should be credited with a pirate's hoard, and the actual presence of a mysterious grave makes it all the more probable; for we know well enough from Treasure Island that, having buried one's treasure, one then buried the burial party. On Polymnie Island, according to the manager, there were an ancient anchor and a grave, and the few who visited the grave had been frightened away by a ghost.

I could not find the anchor but I found the grave, marked only by two pieces of bar-iron riveted together in the form of a cross. It lay in an open space under a casuarina tree so I brought my gear from the dinghy, lit a fire, and settled down for the night. As dusk closed in a weird cry shook me not a little, just as the pirates on Treasure Island had been shaken by the cries of Ben Gunn. Then I remembered that the manager had spoken of wild goats on Polymnie Island. Mosquitoes were the next worry. Having changed from shorts to slacks and rolled down my sleeves I lit a pipe to defend my face and fell to musing upon the grave and what lay beneath. Even if no murder had been done, supposing one of one's crew had died what better place to bury him than on top of the hoard as a deterrent to squeamish treasure hunters?

I piled on more logs. By the light of the fire I could just make out the grave. Glancing in its direction I realized I was being watched, watched by two hideous, goggle eyes that regarded me with a cold, fixed, expressionless stare. They were nearly a foot from the ground and in front of the eyes two great pincer claws waved slowly but menacingly as if feeling for the victim that the eyes had already detected. The huge land crab, for such it was, made no move as I stood up, nor any further move after I hit him with the back end of a hatchet. Another appeared, to be dealt with in the same way, and then several more. Apart from what their claws might do, the notion of sleeping there under the baleful stares of these creatures became abhorrent; nor would the bodies of those that I had killed, which were already being devoured, long stay their insatiable hunger. Retreating to the hauled-up dinghy I contrived a rough bed with the oars laid across the thwarts. More horrible eyes began staring up at me from the sand, but in the dinghy I was safe from crabs and slept fitfully in spite of the mosquitoes.

Near my bivouac I had seen numerous, well-worn tracks made by the giant land tortoise—game trails, in fact, if a tortoise can be regarded as game. I watched one of the creatures lumbering along but did not attempt to ride him as Frank Bullen reports having done on his walk ashore on Aldabra. He measured his mount as four feet long and two feet six inches wide and affirms that it eventually carried him to 'a fine stream of water, sparkling out of the hillside'. These tortoises are reputed to live for hundreds of years. They have one at Government House, St Helena (or had when we called there in 1960) which is believed to have been about the place when Napoleon was in exile there. Bullen also speaks of a patriarch upon whose back a sailor claimed to have seen inscribed: 'The Ark, Captain Noah. Ararat for orders.'

Once more back at the anchorage off the settlement we found the sea too rough for a pirogue to come alongside with water. Early accounts of Aldabra mention a well of fresh water, but the manager had no knowledge of this, nor of Bullen's 'sparkling stream'. We hung on there waiting to water while wind and sea increased alarmingly. A prudent mariner would have spent the night at sea, for the wind was onshore and fifty yards astern of us the seas were breaking on a coral reef. At the settlement they hoisted a white flag, a warning, as we learnt later, for us to clear out.

Before having done with Aldabra I ought to mention a threat that has been hanging over this strange island, an island that in 1958 few had so much as heard of. Briefly there has been a plan for the R.A.F. to use the island as a staging post to the Far East. At an estimated cost of £20 million a 12,000-foot runway would be built at the eastern end and joined to the living quarters, offices, and stores located on West Island by a road having swing bridges across the passes. Apart from the arguments for and against on strategic grounds there is a strong body of scientific opinion against the plan for reasons summed up by Charles Douglas-Home in an article in *The Times*:

> Aldabra is unique. It is an elevated atoll, which is rare in the Indian Ocean where most atolls are sea-level atolls. The higher the atoll the wider the range of plants and animals which exist upon it and the more valuable it is for scientific study. Aldabra has never been mined for guano and thus, unlike most other Indian Ocean Atolls, it has not been stripped of its vegetation and the pure ecology of it has been largely uncontaminated. Parts of Aldabra have been contaminated by human contact. On West Island there is a small settlement of Seychellois fishermen. Their presence has already resulted in the near extinction of the Flightless Rail from South Island because of the incursion of rats and cats from the settlement. But most of the atoll remains unaffected, particularly the east end where the giant tortoise live, which also provides the largest breeding ground in the Indian Ocean for the frigate birds and one of the few remaining breeding grounds of the green turtle. The scientist's main argument against the establishment of the base, however, is the fact that except for those areas contaminated by the settlement, the rest of the island is undisturbed. Thus Aldabra provides a unique opportunity for scientists to study the island's ecosystem and the ways in which it has evolved over centuries without being affected by any outside influence.

To get back to the boat. As I have said we stupidly hung on there throughout an anxious night. As I watched apprehensively the white water close astern of us, Jim expounded the novel theory that our position was nothing like so bad as it looked. We would be most likely, he said, to drag at high water, in which case *Mischief* would be washed over the coral reef and would only be wrecked on the comparatively harmless sandy beach beyond! By morning the wind had dropped and we all went ashore for a last meal of turtle's eggs, meat, and fish provided by the manager's hospitable wife. By evening the sea, too, had gone down and the pirogue came off with our water which we manhandled on board with buckets. Amid cheers and waves from the friendly Seychelles we sailed away.

CHAPTER XV

THE RED SEA AND HOMEWARDS

O UR COURSE TOOK US WEST of the main group of the Seychelles. On a day of exceptional clearness the bold silhouette of Mahé, the principal island, showed above the horizon when over fifty miles away. That night, still, warm, moonlit, we stole quietly past Bird Island, only eight feet high, a white beach, trees, and the light from a solitary hut, endowing it with romance. By dawn we had Denis Island abeam, as low and flat as Bird Island, but having on it a lighthouse; in 1892 it was cultivated, covered with trees, and inhabited. That was the last Indian Ocean island we were to see; the next land sighted was Cape Guarda-fui on the horn of Africa, after a calm uneventful passage of thirty days. We scraped and varnished the beams inside the cabin, black-leaded the stove, scaled and painted the anchor and its winch, and fitted new light screens. Jim finished carving the new name-board, and some genius, Gerry I think, made a rotator for the log, the last of several having been taken by a shark. He carved it from wood, giving it the necessary correctly shaped fins, and filled the inside with lead. After a little adjustment to the length of the line it recorded pretty accurately.

We raised the Guardafui light on the night of March 19th and ran up the Gulf of Aden escorted by two sharks who were in turn accompanied by their pilot fish. The sharks were strangely bright blue in colour but they were not a species new to science, they merely enjoyed rubbing off what was left of our anti-fouling. Arriving at Aden on a Sunday night, bemused by the multitude of lights, ships, oiling buoys, and whatnot, we anchored well clear until the Monday morning when a pilot took us to a berth off the Post Office.

Aden was no longer the drowsy place that I remembered from visits in the 'thirties when bound to India—a place that came to life only when a mailboat disgorged its passengers for a brief sightseeing tour, that boasted the one dingy hotel where for sixpence one could see a mermaid, or in other words a dugong. The oil refinery across the bay and extensions to the harbour had changed all that. We were told that 500 ships called every month, mainly for bunkering. Messrs Luke and Thomas, the shipping agents, looked after us and we were watered by their water-boat without charge. The port authorities, on the other hand, took their pound of flesh in the way of light dues, etc., the first port in which such charges had been levied against *Mischief*. While walking about in Aden I had a momentary fit of vertigo which later had significance. It lasted only a second and I attributed it to the sun, although at that time of year Aden was still comparatively cool.

We were just too late to expect an easy passage up the Red Sea. By April the southerly winds that prevail during the winter months are failing. We could expect favourable winds for about half the 1200-odd miles, thereafter we should have to beat against fresh northerly winds. At Durban they had warned us in all seriousness against Red Sea pirates—such is the enchantment that distance lends to a scene. Possibly if the crew of a small boat were imprudent enough to anchor off some small village on the Arabian coast they might find the natives hostile. We had no intention of stopping anywhere on the way if it could be avoided. Even without pirates the Red Sea provides enough problems for the small-boat sailor—the stream of shipping, strong currents, baffling winds, steep seas, scattered reefs, and only partially lit shores. Another navigational hazard is caused by refraction. On one occasion a light with a range of fourteen miles was seen when we were thirty-seven miles distant. The Brothers, two islands at the northern end about 200 feet high, have been seen at a distance of 100 miles. Thus, owing to the displacement of the horizon, sights, particularly sun sights, are liable to considerable error.

Sailing from Aden on March 27th we went along at a good clip and at dusk next day we passed Perim. That night I woke up feeling fearfully giddy, unable to stand without holding on to something, and vomiting. A few days later I felt strong enough to take my watch, but sights had to be taken sitting down and any quick movement of the head threw one off balance. In the course of the passage matters slowly improved, yet on reaching Lymington three months later I still felt weak and out of balance. Time the great healer, aided by a specialist who had diagnosed a lesion of the labyrinth, affected a cure, but not

Giant land tortoise awaiting shipment in pen at Aldabra

The lagoon, Aldabra

before I had reached such a low ebb as to put *Mischief* up for sale. Fortunately nobody wanted her except as a gift. Having recovered I felt ashamed of this piece of treachery and thankful that *Mischief*, clever as she was at sea, could not read advertisements.

At that stage of the voyage, enjoying a fair southerly wind, we could lay the desired course and had only to keep the stream of ships in sight. The skipper could very well have stayed in his bunk. The log book, in which we recorded ships in sight, showed a total of between twenty and thirty every day. Having run 400 miles in five days, by April 1st we had the 800-foot-high Island of Jabal al Tair abeam, but these easy days of rapid progress were drawing to an end. In about the latitude of Port Sudan the southerly wind died to be replaced almost at once by a stiff northerly blow that soon lashed up a short, steep sea. We now began to make long boards, trying if possible to avoid crossing the shipping lane at night. Standing over to the Arabian side we made out one night the loom of Jedda, and on the next tack towards Africa we had ahead of us the granite peaks of the Berenice Range.

This mountain range lies inland of the justly named Foul Bay, a wide bay thickly studded with rocks and reefs. Here our navigation proved badly askew. We were on the starboard tack steering northwest, confident of weathering Ras Banas, the northern arm of the bay, when over the starboard quarter we saw breaking water. We were already well inside Foul Bay. Going about we steered east with a man aloft who presently saw dead ahead another long line of white water. Thoroughly agitated I stayed on deck until Foul Bay and its horrors were well astern of us. We had now crossed the Red Sea twice and had made good about ten miles to the north. Had it not been for a lucky break in the weather pattern we might still be there. In the next few days a light south-easterly wind brought us to Shadwan Island, the noted seamark at the end of the Red Sea proper and the beginning of the long, narrow Gulf of Suez. It is the crux of the passage, for the prevailing wind is north-westerly, blowing straight through the narrow Strait of Gubal at the entrance to the Gulf. The strait has a navigable width of less than seven miles. Sure enough, out of a clear sky, a moderate gale from north-west descended upon us as soon as Shadwan Island came in sight. We were bashing into it, reefed right down, when one of those short, steep seas curled over and broke on deck, smashing a pane in the skylight as well as one of the twin booms and the deck locker. This glass pane was pretty thick but since then plate glass has been fitted in the skylight. When two seams in the mainsail opened we had to set the trysail and with that sail we had no hope of beating through the Strait of Gubal.

When one door closes, another opens. In this case it was the back-door entrance to the Gulf of Suez by way of the narrow channels west of Shadwan and Gubal Islands. Keeping a look-out aloft for reefs, which are easily seen except when the sun is low, we found sheltered water and anchored for the night off a desolate open beach. The chart names the place Port Endeavour and it is marked by one flat-roofed house in which nobody lives. In this peaceful haven we effected what repairs were needed. Having passed west of Gubal Island we emerged in the gentler winds and seas of the Gulf of Suez, delighted at having thus cheated those malevolent Straits.

For the most part the Gulf of Suez is little more than ten miles wide and the shipping appeared to be even more heavily concentrated. We had to tack pretty well all the way, so that at night, not wishing to make too free with the shore, we were obliged to cross and recross the shipping lane. The 150 miles to Suez took us six days and in the nar-rowest part of the Gulf, when for a day and a half it blew hard, we had to reef right down. Arrived in Suez Bay we anchored off Green Island, miles away from the shore, so fearful were we of intruding upon the Canal entrance and the busy shipping. Perhaps in the course of a day or two we might have plucked up enough courage to draw nearer to the centre of things, but that evening a roving bumboat-man with an eye to business drew alongside. When everything and everybody appears or is suspected to be hostile the least show of friendship is accepted with fervour. We welcomed this man as a brother and delivered our-selves into his hands. At the Quarantine station, where he at once took us, we were soon dealt with by the port doctor and the police.

Our doubts about our reception were owing to the ill-fated Suez affair, for we were there in time to reap the aftermath. These doubts were well founded. We found ourselves objects of suspicion, but the worst result of the affair from our point of view was that there were no longer any European shipping agents at Suez to arrange for our tran-sit through the Canal. Difficulties arose about my going ashore and finally, at the suggestion of our friendly bumboat-man, I left it to him to arrange our clearance with the Canal authorities.

No sooner said than done. By next morning we had the necessary papers and attached to them our agent's bill for £27. The correct figure should have been something less than £10. He must have felt, like Clive, astonished at his own moderation, for he had us neatly impaled. Pay or stay; either we paid and went or remained stewing in Suez. The one-sided argument raged till midday when the arrival of the Canal pilot showed that at least we should get what we paid for. So with something less than urbanity I handed over the money. But our cup was not quite full; there was still a trifling sum of misery to be added to the foot of our account. About an hour later, when we were in the Canal, Douglas discovered the loss of eight gold sovereigns, worth, I suppose, about £40. They had been in the pocket of a suit in the cabin and we had little doubt about who had them. Up to the time of his presenting his bill we had been altogether too friendly with the bumboat-man and his myrmidons whom we had allowed to roam all over the boat. One could not but admire the keenness of their scent for what was worth having and the sleight of hand by which they had secured it. There was nothing to be done. No one in Suez would believe our story, much less take any action.

After spending the night at Geneffe at the entrance to the Little Bitter Lake we arrived next day at Ismailia where we anchored again. There we had welcome showers and learnt the unwelcome news that all our mail had been returned to sender. A fresh pilot took us on to Port Said and we implored him to find us a quiet berth where we could lie for a few days to refit. Accordingly we went alongside the Esso oil berth short of Port Said so that the pilot could telephone the Canal office to ask where we could lie. We never saw him again. The Esso watchman, a rough type, told us to shove off, and after some telephoning on our own behalf we were told to moor in Sherif basin. A less quiet berth could hardly have been found. We lay alongside a trading schooner surrounded by lighters full of onions where the police promptly arrived and put a guard on board. For the next two days we were held incommunicado with nothing to do but sleep and nothing to look at but onions. Through the kind intervention of a man called Marco from one of the shipping agents we were at length given shore passes but our policeman still lived on board. Life became more pleasant when we were allowed to move to the Club Nautique at Port Fuad opposite Port Said. The Club, of course, was dead, all its dinghies and speed boats lying around sunk, but we lay alone in a little basin surrounded by green lawns. We now got some work done, sent up the topmast, and prepared to sail.

From Port Said to Gibraltar is roughly 2000 miles and the really remarkable feature about our passage was that it took two months. Expecting to do it in one hop in the course of a month, we found ourselves forced to put in at Malta, the half-way mark, to refresh. *Mischief* had been there before, had in fact spent five years there, from 1949 to 1954, in the hands of a Maltese ship chandler who now paid us a visit. They had not been happy years for her. Before Ernle Bradford bought her and took her to Majorca shortly before turning her over to me, she had been grossly neglected.

Unlike the eastern half of the Mediterranean, in the western half we had plenty of wind, but it nearly always came from ahead and sometimes in such strength that we had to seek shelter. Having been pushed over to the African coast we had to lie up behind Cape Farina in the Gulf of Tunis, in company with a number of other small craft, while a westerly gale blew itself out. With the help of a few days of easterly winds we then made a great leap forward until another westerly gale drove us to shelter in a cove near Caba de Gata east of Almeria. Three times we had to anchor in small bays along the Spanish coast. On one occasion, having prematurely left our snug hole to try conclusions with the west wind and east-going current, after beating for twenty-four hours we were happy to reach the coast again five miles east of the anchorage we had quitted. Meantime ships that had passed us in the Eastern Mediterranean homeward bound now began to repass us outward bound. One of these on recognising us again gave us an encouraging cheer. She happened to be a ship I knew, the *Jan Olden van Barneveldt*, one of a large convoy that had sailed from Liverpool to India in 1941. She was a fine passenger ship that had only recently been requisitioned, with all her peace-time chefs and stewards on board and stuffed full of the sort of food and wine demanded by first-class passengers on the Atlantic run. The purser, who abhorred as much as we did, the thought that all these good things might go to the bottom unused, was easily persuaded to let us consume them. It reminded me of a similar precaution that had been taken by the famous climber Mummery and his guide Bergener on the Furggen ridge of the Matterhorn; 'Immediately in front, the long, pitiless slabs, ceaselessly swept by whizzing, shrieking fragments of all sorts and sizes, suggested to Burgener—who had a most proper and prudent objection to every form of waste—that it would be well to drink our Bouvier, and consume our other provisions, before any less fitting fate should overtake them.'

At Gibraltar where we arrived on July 3rd, we lay in the 'Cormorant' camber, normally reserved for vessels of the Royal Navy. *Mischief* was once more on familiar ground, for in 1954, her maiden voyage as far as I was concerned, she had lain in the same berth for some weeks while I sought to replace the crew that had brought her from Majorca and then left. The Rock, its apes, and its caves, was thus familar to me and I had time to spare to repaint the deck and the topsides. Jim Lovegrove left us here to attend to his growing family, but for the last leg to Lymington, which we accomplished in twenty days, we needed no substitute.

Warned by my bitter experience in 1954, the result of ignorance, we sailed well out into the Atlantic 200 miles west of Portugal before trying to head north. In 1954, with a scratch crew culled from the Gibraltar garrison, we had attempted to beat north up the coast against the so-called Portuguese Trades. After eighteen days, having reached somewhere near Oporto, the crew, who had had enough, forced me to put in and land them. This time our strategy was successful. We dodged the north wind and soon picked up Westerlies. As I say, we thus circumvented the winds of heaven, though one might well ask, like Captain MacWhirr, how did we know that the winds we had dodged were in fact blowing?

The moderate gales and immoderate rain we met in the Channel assured us that we were home again in time to enjoy an English summer. We reached Lymington after a voyage of 22,000 miles and an absence of thirteen months. A voyage in which we had suffered defeat, and from which I brought back only a piece of red coral, some hardwon experience, and many happy memories.

Tilman's 'Grace Darling'

◆

Janet Verasanso

IN EARLY MAY 1951 the British people were either looking forward eagerly to the Festival of Britain or wondering whether (despite the draconian currency restrictions) it might not be a good moment to take a holiday abroad. My husband, Ernle Bradford, and I belonged to the latter category. In anticipation of the crowds and incessant media reportage, we sold our possessions and bought a small ten-ton ex-racing Dutch boeier named *Mother Goose*, which we hoped would take us through the French canals to the quieter delights of the Mediterranean. To be able to cruise this sea, visiting the Renaissance cities of Tuscany and the ancient sites of Greece, had been my dream since childhood. To do so in one's own boat, especially after the privations of the war and immediate post-war period, seemed almost unbelievable.

Ernle had spent much of the war in the Mediterranean as a navigating officer aboard destroyers and was keen to revisit the area in peacetime; while for me sailing and maritime history had become the abiding passions of my life. In 1950 I was fortunate to become the first woman to win the Little Ship Club Claude Worth Trophy for seamanship and navigation. Together we formed a capable team, ready for the adventure ahead, though there were those who doubted the wisdom of taking a boat with a two-foot draught and leeboards anywhere out of sight of land.

Ernle resigned his editorship of an antiques magazine. Armed with contracts to supply articles for several publications, on 3 May we set off from Chichester to cross the Channel. We spent three unforgettable years exploring the Mediterranean, spending the first winter in Malta, where we were enthusiastically welcomed by the Navy and their bored British wives eager for new topics of conversation; and the second in Palermo, where our arrival coincided with Warner Brothers' filming of *The Master of Ballantrae*, starring Errol Flynn. A sailing friend immediately found work for us on the production; the filming over, we returned to Malta.

Here we discovered the pilot cutter *Mischief* lying disconsolate and unloved, moored between two buoys in Kalkara Creek off Valletta Harbour. She was my idea of a sturdy, seaworthy craft, built for work in any conditions. Her lines were sweet and utterly traditional. Who had sailed her to Malta remains a mystery to me; the Mediterranean was certainly an unlikely choice of cruising ground for a vessel designed for the western approaches to the Bristol Channel. She belonged to a local ship chandler who had taken a liking to our ship *Mother Goose*. After some hard bargaining we became *Mischief*'s new owners.

She was not in the best condition but thanks to assistance from John Illingworth, that giant of the ocean-racing scene, who was stationed in Malta at the time, we were able to put to sea with the idea of sailing her to Palma de Mallorca, and thence to England the following summer. Beset by alternating calms and squalls—not the best weather to show off her sailing abilities, but typical of most of the Med—we reached Mallorca in mid-August, mooring stern to the palatial Palma yacht club and alongside *Iolaire*, owned by Bobby Somerset, one of the founders of the Royal Ocean Racing Club. After several days in Palma we sailed westward along the southern coast to Puerto Andratx in company with *Iolaire*. Here *Mischief* was laid up for the winter with another Bristol Channel pilot cutter alongside. For us it was time to return to London; after almost three years in the Mediterranean, we had to think about reality and a winter of concentrated work.

While we were in London we were approached by Bobby Somerset with the news that an acquaintance who had crewed aboard *Iolaire* was looking for a suitable ship, complete with experienced crew, to take him round the southernmost tip of South America to Patagonia. There he planned to cross the largely unexplored southern ice field and enjoy a (very) quick swim in the extremely chilly waters of Lake Argentino. This person turned out to be the renowned and intrepid mountaineer H. W. 'Bill' Tilman, whose exploits with Eric Shipton on Nanda Devi in 1934 and on the Everest expeditions of 1935 and 1938 were already legendary amongst aficionados. Personally, I was too young to be aware of them, while Ernle had no interest in the subject. We therefore had no forewarning that Tilman was a man only truly happy in appallingly uncomfortable living conditions, and a firm believer in middle-class Victorian values—values from which, like many others, we had firmly moved away. After some correspondence we arranged to meet for supper in a small Greek restaurant on the King's Road, Chelsea. Our meeting proceeded fairly well, and I found myself eager to experience those frozen wastes. We had at that early meeting no inkling of Tilman's visceral distrust of women—hardly surprising, as he had of course not yet written the passage of his first sailing book, *Mischief in Patagonia*, quoting an unknown Chinese sage to the effect that discord is not sent down from Heaven but is brought about by Woman. Ernle made it very clear during supper that we sailed as a couple, and Tilman undertook to let us know soon if he wished to buy *Mischief*.

It is unlikely that she was the only suitable boat for sale at that moment, and we were unsure if we wished to part with her. Despite his unexpressed misgivings about my gender he did, however, decide to acquire her, and together we sketched out an initial plan. *Mischief* would be hauled out at the yard in Palma, surveyed, and (if she passed) made ready for her voyage. We would oversee this task, Ernle as captain and myself as bosun. Two young mountaineers would join the boat in Gibraltar to make up the full complement.

In the spring of 1954 *Mischief* was hauled out at Ballester's shipyard in Palma, and a great deal of work carried out, including, among other improvements, some new planking, sails, rigging, caulking, stiffening in way of the mast and a thorough overhaul and strengthening throughout. It seemed endless. Some of the original cement was removed from the bilges and no rot was found. Ballester's yard could not have been more appropriate for her refit as their work largely relied on repairing the wooden fishing fleet. Their elderly foreman, Guiem, was a hugely experienced shipwright in whom we had total confidence.

Ernle, Tilman and I worked and lived aboard *Mischief*. It can only be described as a working relationship, but we appeared to cope satisfactorily. Days spent refitting on board were compensated by lively evenings ashore with locals and visiting yachts, on which Tilman never joined us. He later admitted that he was inexperienced during this period; nevertheless, he exhibited a strange inability to leave perfectly functioning equipment alone—the camera on loan from the National

Geographic was one of his casualties, the Primus another. We found it exasperating trying to find something for him to do. I suggested he might sew some cockpit cushions, and this kept him busy for many hours; that he accepted this instruction from a woman is astonishing. On one occasion, showing characteristic insensitivity, Tilman told Ernle and me that he despised yachtsmen and only mountaineers received his unqualified admiration. Tension continued to build on board. We fervently hoped that when we got to sea, matters would improve.

Eventually the day arrived when *Mischief* slid down the ways. Her crew was augmented by the arrival of Jack, an ex-*Iolaire* hand, and Guy, a friendly person with a lot of willingness and some sailing experience whom we had met in Palermo the year before. A few stores were brought aboard and safely stowed, including food sufficient for four days. If food became short we knew there were plenty of ports along the Spanish coast where we could put in for further supplies. The distance between Palma and Gibraltar is approximately 450 nautical miles, but of course the winds are unreliable. Tilman, disregarding Ernle's advice that we might encounter days of calm, calculated that we would make daily runs of at least a hundred miles. We all settled down to a routine of watches and took turns to cook and wash up.

The atmosphere on board was quietly friendly, but Tilman normally remained silent and aloof. It was becoming increasingly clear that he felt I was an intrusion. Though he generously referred to me as 'Grace Darling' in *Mischief in Patagonia*, acknowledging that I could hand, reef and steer, he resented my presence. On one occasion, when we were down to our last piece of fresh meat, it was my turn to cook. I made a beef stew. I would be the first to admit that I am not overly interested in cooking, but can produce an adequate stew. Tilman was at the helm. On receiving his bowl he took a mouthful and threw the rest overboard. We were all dumbfounded. The next day Guy made a similar, but vegetarian, dish. Tilman, again steering, looked at me, declared that he felt relieved we had a cook on board, and thanked God for Guy. In his introduction to *Mischief in Patagonia* he remarks that, 'perhaps one of the few remarks I had made had not been well chosen.' There was no need for him even to have mentioned it; perhaps it demonstrates his psychological complexity as a man and chronicler.

Light airs or no wind at all became our lot during the entire voyage from Palma to Gibraltar, and our four days' supply of food was running dangerously low. Ernle asked if we could put in to a port to get both fuel and food, but Tilman obstinately (and inexplicably, as he was keen to get to Gibraltar as soon as possible to load stores for the voyage to South America) refused. Finally, at 0700 on the eighth day (Tilman records a voyage of ten days) we rounded the Rock of Gibraltar and tied up to a pontoon. The ship's stores amounted to plenty of water and half a jar of marmalade. On the other side of the pontoon lay the yacht *Beyond*, with Tom Worth and his wife Anne, who were on the last leg of their round-the-world cruise. We explained our situation and inquired if there was a baker nearby. They very kindly offered us a loaf, apologising that it had been purchased the day before. At that moment Tilman came up from below, took the loaf in his hands, turned it over, declared, 'It's stale,' and in front of the Worths standing in their cockpit and the rest of *Mischief*'s crew, threw it overboard.

It was an exhibition I found impossible to ignore. I lost my temper, told him that I could go no further and that I was not a paid hand but went to sea for the love of sailing in good company. Ernle's feelings totally coincided with mine; he and the other crew members followed me ashore on the same day. Tilman made no reply. We were clearly deficient in Victorian ideals, not made of the Right Stuff, and (in my case) despicably female. I believe that though his subsequent sailing career spanned twenty-three years, I remain the only woman to have sailed with him.

In *Mischief in Patagonia*, Tilman seemed content to lay the blame on me by referencing the cooking incident; even going so far as to feel sorry for Ernle who, Tilman suggested, had no option but to leave the boat, as 'a wife's counsel is bad, but he who will not take it is mad'. I believe that some of his later crew problems on that voyage, and indeed others, may have stemmed from his inability to comprehend that other people might possibly have different systems of interpersonal behaviour.

In later years I often crewed for both Bobby Somerset and Henry Denham, then Rear Commodore of the Royal Cruising Club (which I joined) before owning two boats in the Pacific and another, shared with two others, in the Caribbean, eventually downsizing to a Vertue and lastly a Corribee, both of which I sailed in the Med, parting with the latter in 1995.

In retrospect it seems almost incredible that Tilman, who was so inept in the yard and on the voyage to Gibraltar, had within a matter of months become a true sailor, fearlessly mastering the intricacies of traditional ocean navigation and deep-sea sailing. He remains a colossus among the many heroes of the twentieth century, whose laconic sense of humour and wit lay deeply buried in his day-to-day life, but was brought out most amusingly in excellent and frequently very frank books, which once started are difficult to put down. The final paragraph in *Mischief in Patagonia* explains his philosophy: that loyalty to the ship and enterprise in hand should be put before one's own feelings. The fact that no such stern resolve stiffened my spine no doubt reinforced his belief that I was a five-star perpetuator of the sins of Eve. It is hard not to conclude that he must have breathed a quiet Victorian sigh of relief as I walked away down the pontoon.

H. W. TILMAN

The Collected Edition

FOR THE FIRST TIME SINCE THEIR ORIGINAL APPEARANCE, all fifteen books by H. W. Tilman are being published as single volumes, with all their original photographs, maps and charts. Forewords and afterwords by those who knew him, or who can bring their own experience and knowledge to bear, complement his own understated writing to give us a fuller picture of the man and his achievements. A sixteenth volume is the 1980 biography by J. R. L. Anderson, *High Mountains and Cold Seas*. The books will appear in pairs, one each from his climbing and sailing eras, in order of original publication, at quarterly intervals from September 2015:

www.tilmanbooks.com